EXODUS II
Let My People Go

By Steve Lightle
with Eberhard Muehlan and Katie Fortune

Published by Hunter Books
City of Light
201 McClellan Road
Kingwood, Texas 77339, U.S.A.

The original of this work was published in the German language by Verlag Schulte & Gerth, Emmelusstr. 31, 6334 Asslar, West Germany.

Published by Hunter Books, City of Light, 201 McClellan Road, Kingwood, TX 77339. Printed in USA.

Scripture quotations are taken from:
New American Standard Bible (NAS) ©The Lockman Foundation 1960, 1962, 1963, 1968, 1971, 1972, 1973, 1975, and 1977.

The Holy Bible: New International Version (NIV) ©1978 by New York International Bible Society. Used by permission of Zondervan Bible Publishers.

The Authorized King James Version (KJV). All Scripture quotations are taken from the New American Standard Bible unless otherwise stated.

ISBN 0-917726-56-1

PREFACE

Over a period of ten years, dozens of people have said to me, "Steve, why don't you write a book about all the things that have happened to you and how the Lord has led you?"

While I knew deep in my heart that one day I would write a book, I would brush off the suggestions saying, "There are enough books on the market already." I knew it would only be written when the Lord would tell me to do so. It must be in His timing.

Then in November of 1982, Dov and Tehilah Chaikin came to our house in Jerusalem one morning for coffee. The Lord had given them a "rhema" (a personal word from the Word) from Isaiah 43:16-19 that they were "not to call to mind the former things" (the first exodus of the Jews out of Egypt) but that the Lord was going to do "something new" (the second exodus of the Jews, this time out of Russia).

While we were discussing this, they said they had felt the Lord wanted me to know that it was time to write a book about this second exodus. We said a short prayer and they left.

I went to my study and wrote "BOOK" on my prayer list just to remind me to pray about it. About an hour later while my wife, Judy, was preparing lunch, I began to read aloud to her our Old Testament reading for the day which happened to be Jeremiah 29 and 30. As I read the first three verses of Jeremiah 30, I had to shout for joy!

"The word which came to Jeremiah from the Lord, saying, 'Thus says the Lord, the God of Israel, "Write all the words which I have spoken to you in a

book. *For, behold, days are coming,"* declares the Lord, *"when I will restore the fortunes of My people Israel and Judah." The Lord says, "I will also bring them back to the land that I gave to their forefathers, and they shall possess it" ' "* (Jeremiah 30:1-3).

God could not have spoken any more clearly to me if He had been standing there in person speaking to me. This was the confirmation I needed to write the book. Not only did it confirm the task, but the third verse of the chapter confirmed the subject of the book.

When I read on and came to the last verse it confirmed that the book was to be written "in the last days:" *"The fierce anger of the Lord will not turn back, until He has performed, and until He has accomplished the intent of His heart; In the latter days you will understand this"* (Jeremiah 30:24).

So Judy, my friend Matt McLallin (who lives with us), and I sat right down to write the book. Nineteen pages later I realized that there is a great difference between speaking and writing. Between that revelation and Matt and Judy's uncontrollable laughter at my efforts I finally said, "Lord, I quit! If You want this book written, You'll have to send me some help."

And that's exactly what He did. Eberhard Muehlan not only researched and compiled all of Part II, but he also was called by God to use his writing talents in preparing the original German manuscript. In the truest sense of the expression, he proved to be an answer to prayer. To God be all the glory!

INTRODUCING THE LIGHTLE FAMILY

Steve Lightle lives in Jerusalem with his wife, Judy, and two daughters, Lynn and Michele. A former businessman from Seattle, Washington, Steve and his family attended St. Luke's Episcopal Church in Seattle. In 1973 Steve moved his family to Braunschweig, West Germany, the city that admitted Hitler into German citizenship from Austria.

Steve lived in Brussels, Belgium from 1976 to 1981 where he worked as the European Director of the Full Gospel Business Men's Fellowship International. He has traveled and ministered in every country behind the Iron Curtain except Bulgaria and Albania. He has been on four extensive trips in the Soviet Union. For the next two and one-half years Steve was with Eastern European Bible Mission, working behind the Iron Curtain.

In 1974, during a six and one-half day fast in Braunschweig, West Germany, Steve received a vision of God's plan to bring the two and one-half to three million Jewish people out of the Soviet Union and return them to the land of Israel.

Steve travels and speaks extensively around the world and now the message that burns in his heart is God's plan for the return of the Jews to Israel in these last days.

ACKNOWLEDGMENTS

I want to express my thanks to all the people the Lord sent my way to help:

To Eberhard Muehlan who first wrote the basic manuscript in German...

To Wolfgang Dick for translating the German manuscript into English...

To Katie Fortune for editing and rewriting the English manuscript...

To Don Fortune for his diligent help in coordinating work...

To Carrie Wingfield and Sue Duncan for typing and retyping and retyping the manuscript...

To my wife, Judy, and my daughters, Lynn and Michele, for their love and support in this project and for allowing me to invest the many hours that were necessary to work on the manuscript.

To God be the glory!

Contents

PART I

THE VOICE IN THE WILDERNESS

CHAPTER 1

AT THE RUSSIAN SYNAGOGUE

Sleeping in a hotel bed in Russia was not unusual for me, since I had been traveling in various countries behind the Iron Curtain for three years. But this night I could not fall asleep and was tossing back and forth. The experience at the synagogue that day had just been one of the most tremendous ones I had ever had. My mind kept going over the events of the day, and I could not get to sleep.

The day had not begun as well as it had ended. We had started out early to go back and forth across town by bus and tram to make various contacts, all without success. By ten o'clock that morning we were back in the hotel. My feet were hurting, and I threw myself on the bed and stared at the ceiling with disappointment.

What did all this mean? Had the Lord really sent me on this journey, or had this all been my own idea? As I began to quiet down, the Holy Spirit started speaking to my heart in the way I have known Him to do so often, "Get up, walk out of the hotel, and go to the synagogue of this town to proclaim the Gospel!"

"But Lord, preaching the Gospel is not the most popular thing to do in Russia, and on top of that You want me to do it in the synagogue?"

"Jesus preached in the synagogue, Paul preached in the synagogue, and you can do it as well," came the answer.

I groaned as I thought about my sore feet. "Jesus, it will only work if You show us the way and come with us, leading us every step of the way." That much I knew. If Jesus motivates us and guides the endeavor, it will be successful.

I walked over into the next room to see my friend Hans. A Norwegian, he was traveling with me because he could speak Russian well and serve as an interpreter. Hans looked like a Russian, and he spoke the language so perfectly because he had learned it in Russia, that he was always mistaken for a Russian. There is a kind of place in the Soviet Union where only foreign tourists can purchase things. It's called a Buroska. We were entering a Buroska one time and he made the mistake of speaking in Russian and they threw us out. They wouldn't let us come in because they said that we were Russians. We had to produce our passports and prove to them that indeed we were foreigners.

"Hans," I said, "the Lord told me that we are to walk out of the hotel and go to the synagogue to preach the Gospel."

"Forget it!" he said emphatically. "I'm not going

with you. I'm not going to walk anywhere. I have been tramping for hours through this city trying to find what you were looking for, and we never found it. How in the world are we going to find a synagogue?"

"Look!" I said, "I know we are supposed to go."

Hans was obviously not excited about going out again. But knowing me and my persistence when I know the Lord has spoken, he felt it was better to obey the Lord rather than cater to his own "flesh."

"But I am not going to walk!" Hans protested. "We'll either take a taxi or we'll take a tram. The city's too large. Besides we have no idea where to find this synagogue."

"Nope," I said. "We're walking! The Lord specifically said to 'walk'."

"Okay," he agreed reluctantly.

So, we left the hotel and started walking down the street. We had no idea where the synagogue would be, or even if there was one. But after walking about ten blocks, we found a little old lady standing on a street corner. One thing Hans had told me was, "You never ask a young person directions in Russia. You always find a little old lady and ask her because then you know she's not with the KGB and she won't report you."

"Excuse me, please," Hans said to the lady. "Can you tell us where the synagogue is?" And she looked at us like we were just as ignorant as could be. "Where is the synagogue?" he asked again. And she just pointed directly across the street from us. And sure enough, there it was--a huge synagogue! It was the only synagogue in the city, even though there were more than 165,000 registered Jews. The Lord had led us directly to the place.

So we crossed the street. The synagogue was very run down on the outside. You could barely make out what it was. On the gate was a Star of David that was almost rusted out. It was hardly noticeable. The whole area was overgrown, not kept well at all.

There were three men sitting on a little bench outside the gate. They stood up and motioned to us, "Shh, be quiet, don't say anything." And they motioned to us to go in through the gate. So we walked in without saying anything to them, and we walked along the side of the synagogue and came to a side door. One of the men followed us and motioned to us to get in the door without saying anything. So we slipped in the door. When we got inside, an old Russian Jewish man just grabbed me and kissed me right on the lips, as is their custom. Then a few seconds later, one of the other men slipped in, and then the other one. But when I spoke, they realized that we were foreigners. They became frightened, cold, and stiff because they didn't know who we might be. But they pointed us to where the service was and we went in.

It was the Sabbath, and as we entered we found ourselves in the midst of the Jewish worship service in a beautiful sanctuary. The people, of course, realized that we were strangers. They were cautious and not too friendly. There we were, sitting among many Jews. I was curiously looking around and questioned, "Lord, what comes next? After all, You have led us here."

When the worship service was over, the people stood around in groups and talked. The men were on the ground floor and the women remained in the balcony. All of a sudden an older man who handles the responsibilities of a rabbi apparently observed us and came over and started the conversation. "May I show you around the synagogue?"

"Oh, that would be wonderful!" I replied. It was the first sign of friendliness since we had entered the synagogue service.

"Where you are standing is exactly at the acoustical center of this beautiful synagogue," he explained at the beginning of his guided tour. "If you were to sing at this exact place," he went on, "the sound would rise to the dome and be carried into every corner of the building. Everyone could hear you clearly!"

"Really!" I exclaimed. "Do you mind if I sing something now?"

"If you know how to sing, please do so," he answered.

Well, it's a good thing that he did not know me. My wife, Judy, used to say that the only song that I could sing was to make a joyful noise unto the Lord. But at this moment I recognized the opportunity that the Lord had given me and dared to open my mouth. The anointing of the Holy Spirit welled up in me and I began to sing in a beautiful language that I had never learned. The melodious song I was singing, in a tongue unknown to me, rose to the dome of the synagogue and was carried into every corner of the building.

Suddenly, all conversation stopped, and everyone stared at us. Deeply moved, the rabbi turned to Hans in amazement saying, "Only God knows what this man is singing!" Little did he know the truth he was saying. For in I Corinthians 14:2 we read that he who speaks in an unknown tongue speaks not unto men, but unto God.

This strange introduction opened the heart of the rabbi and the other men. They invited us for dinner which concluded for them a period of fasting. They served a simple meal of fish and bread and a special drink. We had a wonderful time and after the meal we talked, sang, and danced according to the Jewish custom.

Hans was impressed at how they danced and sang before the Lord, shouted, and clapped their hands. "We don't even do that in our church," he said. "Do you think they would mind if I got up and joined them?"

"Sure, come on, let's go," I said. And we got up and we danced and worshipped and praised the Lord with the men there in the synagogue.

When we sat down Hans said, "This is one of the greatest experiences I've ever had since I accepted Jesus." He was overwhelmed by the fact there was such liberty to worship God.

The cantor of the synagogue had been sitting directly across from me. We had been able to communicate quite well since we both spoke German. I had observed that he had been watching me during this time. Finally he leaned over the table and with his hand in front of his mouth he said, "You act as if you have been saved out of all the problems of this world."

"Well, I have been!" was my immediate answer.

"That's what I thought," he said. "Why don't you tell me about it!"

I moved to his side of the table and began to share. When the other men saw it, they came over and listened to what I had to say. Only the Lord could have prepared and made a situation like this possible. For four and a half hours I shared out of my life and proclaimed the Gospel to them. I explained that through my Jewish mother, who was a believing Christian, I had come to know about Jesus. But it was only five years ago that I had made Him to be my personal Messiah and Lord.

All of the men had fixed their eyes on me and we were oblivious to time as I shared how I had built my own life and career without God. I had built a gas station with a car wash and called it "Dippy Duck Car Wash." It became the center of my life. But one morning Jesus apprehended me and called for a total commitment of my life to Him. I was able to give everything to Him — my life, my family, my business, my car, the gas station, everything. Then He promised to take care of me and my family, to feed us, clothe us, and take care of every need.

Later I met people who were "on fire" for God who shared in a very natural way what Jesus meant to them and how He had changed the way they lived their daily lives. I was fascinated and wanted to live like them. They shared that the Bible promised that we would receive power if we asked Jesus to baptize us in the Holy Spirit. I did pray and I received the power of the Holy Spirit and the ability to praise God in a new language. Without that gift, I could never have won the hearts of the Jewish men in that synagogue.

All this happened in 1970, followed by three years of preparation in which I learned to trust the Word of God in the Bible, to live in the power of the Holy Spirit, and learn to listen to His voice and to be obedient.

In 1973, the Lord led me to Europe. During a six and one-half day fast in Braunschweig, West Germany, the Lord showed me in a vision that He will lead the Jewish people out of Russia. It was after this experience that I began to travel throughout the countries of eastern Europe to get acquainted with the culture, the people, and, most of all, to talk to the Jewish people.

So, here I was, sitting with the Jews in a synagogue and sharing all the changes of my life since my encounter with my Messiah.

The anointing of God in the room was so strong that we did not realize the passing of so much time. It had been four and one-half hours. The men were so moved that they requested to know this God. They knelt down with tears in their eyes. We laid hands on their heads and prayed that they would come to know the living God.

What a touching situation! When God leads people and they are obedient to His Spirit, He can touch hearts regardless of race, nationality, or circumstances.

It was a scene I would never forget.

CHAPTER 2

THE TIME OF PREPARATION

No wonder that after all this excitement I was lying on my hotel bed, unable to get to sleep. In all my ministry I had never seen anything like it. How wonderful the Lord is! How grateful I am that I can live my life with Him as Lord. In reviewing the events of the day in my mind, I was rejoicing about what had happened. It had begun with Jesus speaking to me personally with the challenge to get up and walk to the synagogue. Then, there was His miraculous leading of us right to the place. I had to chuckle as I thought how, even though I cannot sing, I had won the hearts of the Jews by opening my mouth and praising the Lord publicly in tongues. It had opened the door for a bold testimony and a time of prayer for the men with whom we had dined.

Suddenly I realized that every year, every month, yes, almost every day since my spiritual rebirth, had been in preparation for the ministry behind the Iron

Curtain and in particular this experience in the synagogue. Many times the Holy Spirit had given me the boldness to do things which otherwise I surely would not have dared to do.

Once in another city behind the Iron Curtain my interpreter, Gerhard Holtz, and I were to be at a meeting up in the mountains with a group of pastors. As we were going to leave the campground where we were staying to join them, we were impressed by the Holy Spirit not to go. "Don't go now!" He spoke to my heart emphatically. After prayer in the afternoon, we still had the same warning. We prayed again the next morning, and still the answer was, "No — don't go now!"

But at about two o'clock that day, we felt a release to go. We walked several kilometers to the house where the meetings were being held. As we approached, we could hear violins and tamborines and other musical instruments and shouts of praise.

When they saw us, they really rejoiced. "Thank God you did not come until just now," they said. "The secret police have been here right up to an hour ago, checking out all our passports and trying to find out why we are all together in this house."

Had we gone to the meeting any sooner, not only would we have been subject to the arbitrary whims of the secret police, but our presence there could have jeopardized the safety of all the pastors who had gathered there. It is illegal there for such a gathering to take place. The Holy Spirit protected all of us.

I've discovered that it is just as important to know when not to go somewhere as it is to know when to go. In the book of Acts, the Holy Spirit gave such a warning. Just before Paul and Timothy received the call to Macedonia, the Holy Spirit restrained them from going to Asia and then shortly after that they were not permitted by the Holy Spirit to go to Bythinia. *"And they passed through the Phrygian and Galatian region, having been forbidden by the Holy Spirit to speak the word in Asia; and when they had come to Mysia, they were trying to go into Bythinia, and the Spirit of Jesus did not permit them"* (Acts 16:6,7).

Traveling in Russia is not always safe and there have been times when I needed to know how to hear the Lord's voice clearly — to really know what He was saying to do or not to do. I'm so grateful that even in my first encounter with Jesus, I heard His voice.

Perhaps it was necessary for Him to speak firmly to me, for I was so set in my own self-centered, self-achieving ways. And money had become my god.

Even as a child I was interested in making money. I was good at it and I learned how to save money and multiply my assets.

I had my first stock broker when I was eleven years old and by the time I was fifteen, my investments had grown and I was making good money off my stocks and bonds. I had a regular job when I was in my early teens working for a veterinarian. I had more money when I was in the seventh grade than my father made right after the depression when he was married and had three children. I was making sixty dollars a month, a tremendous amount of money at that time for a boy who was in the seventh grade. I felt like the richest kid in the school. I invested most of that money and it began to grow and grow. Money became my security, my god.

I was only seventeen when I went off to Washington State University in Pullman, Washington. My mother gave me a Bible. The last thing I wanted was a Bible. But I loved my mother, so I took it and went off to the university. I was really determined to make my mark in the world.

But my mother told me that a day would come in my life when I would realize that I was a hopeless young man and that there would be no help in my finances, in my money, in the stock broker, or anything else. And that when I broke and began to cry and wondered what was happening to my life, and I recognized in my own heart that I was hopeless, then I was to take this Bible she had handed me, open it, point, begin to read, and that I would find out what I was really looking for to give me satisfaction in my life.

I took the Bible with me, but didn't open it. At school I tucked it away, out of sight.

Things were going along all right for me for awhile. Then one night, while I was studying, a voice began to speak to me. Not audibly. I didn't hear it through my ears but I heard it loudly inside me. This voice began to ask me questions of an eternal nature, questions like, "Why are you on the face of this earth?" I didn't have any answer to that because I didn't know why I was here. Nobody asked me to be born. Life was not my idea. I had no idea what my purpose was here on this earth and I couldn't answer things of an eternal nature.

Then this voice said, "If you were to die right now, is there anything within you that could prolong your life one single second?"

And, of course, my answer to that question was, "No." I knew there was nothing inside of me that could prolong my life if I were to die. My father owned a funeral home and an ambulance service. I had been to more funerals than I cared to remember. I had worked on the ambulance crew and scraped up the bodies of many people who had been killed in automobile accidents. I knew that when you are dead, you are dead. And so I knew that if I died there would be nothing left of me. And all of a sudden I recognized for the first time that I was a hopeless young man. I began to cry.

My father had taught me to be a man and that men don't cry. Yet here I was, crying like a little child. I was crying and wondering, "What am I going to do? What am I going to do? If I die, what's going to happen to me?" I was really seriously confronted with this for the first time. I couldn't stop the voice. I couldn't stop the questions.

And then I thought, "Well, if I can't help myself, maybe there is someone else who can." And then I remembered that my mother had told me--that when this situation happened, when I recognized I was a hopeless young man, that I should read that little Bible she had given me.

I found that Bible and took it in my hands, closed my eyes, and just opened it up. I had a pen in my hand

and I pointed on the page with it and then I opened my eyes. The pen pointed exactly under Matthew 6:33, *"But seek first His kingdom and His righteousness; and all these things shall be added to you."* I thought, "This is really something!" I read again, *"But seek first His kingdom and His righteousness."*

"God, could it possibly be that You are the one who is speaking to me?" I cried out. "God, I don't know how to seek You, I don't know how to come to You. I don't know how to pray. I really don't even know what to do. But, in my own miserable, meager way I ask You to help me."

I was still crying as I read it again. *"But seek first His kingdom and His righteousness."* I just said to myself, "I wonder what His righteousness is?"

And that same voice just boomed through me loudly and said, "That's My Son, Jesus the Messiah, the Son of the God of Abraham, Isaac, and Jacob!"

"Oh, no, God," I said, "if You exist and Jesus does too, and I don't know it, I'm in trouble." Then I said, "If this is true, if this really is You speaking to me, then I want You to prove it to me. Do something in my life to change me right now. Not tomorrow. Not next week. Not next month. Not next year. I want You to change me right now, in this very instant."

And I found that even as I was still crying, something jerked me out of my chair. I was just lifted out of my chair. I did not stand up. Something pulled me out of my chair and stood me up.

In the fraternity house where I lived there was a German exchange student named Arndt. He and I didn't get along with each other at all. Being that he was a German, and because of the Jewish background in my life, there was just no love lost between us. But I went right away to find that young man.

At that time I weighed 286 pounds. I had played football in high school, and even though I wasn't all that tough, I was strong. And here he was, just a little guy. Arndt looked at me and he saw 286 pounds coming at him. He thought, "Oh oh!" I was still crying. He thought it was all over. He put up his fists to defend himself.

"Hey, no, wait a minute," I called to him. "I don't understand this, and I don't expect you to understand it, but I want to tell you something. I like you!"

At that instant I knew that Jesus had changed my life. It says in I John 3:14 that, *"We know that we have passed out of death into life, because we love the brethren."* And I didn't know if he was a brother, but I did know this: all of a sudden there was love in my heart for the first time *ever* for somebody from Germany.

I got so happy. I'll never forget it. I just started yelling: "Jesus is alive! Jesus is alive!" And I went running down the hall. It was study hours, a quiet time in the house when no one is supposed to talk. And I'm running down the hall yelling, "Jesus is alive! Jesus is alive!"

One guy stuck his head out of one of the doors and said, "Shut up, you crazy nut! How do *you* know Jesus is alive?"

And I turned back and yelled at him, "Because He just changed my life!" I just had to tell about it. I told some of my friends and they all thought I'd just flipped out.

For quite awhile, things changed in my life, but not as much as they should have. For a few months I walked with the Lord and then I began to drift away. But once in awhile I would go to church. I even studied a lot about God and my new faith, but my commitment just did not hold. I became, at best, a lukewarm Christian. But God did not give up on me.

CHAPTER 3

SCHOOL OF THE HOLY SPIRIT

The years at "Dippy Duck Car Wash," since I was born again, had not been just a useless transition period, waiting to begin the ministry in the Kingdom of God, but they were a daily "Bible School of the Holy Spirit." In looking back, I recognized that I had learned three basic principles for the challenging ministry behind the Iron Curtain: First - to really get to know the Word of God and deeply depend on it, just as God had said to the young prophet Jeremiah at the beginning of his ministry, "I am watching over My word to perform it." (Jeremiah 1:12) Second - to count on and live with the power of the Holy Spirit. Third - to hear and obey the voice of God as Jesus said in John 10:27, "My sheep hear My voice."

These principles must be learned by those who wish to be in an effective ministry for the Lord.

What a tremendous hunger for the Word of God had developed in me in those early years. Very quickly I experienced God's faithfulness. He confirms His Word, if we walk in obedience. In the Bible I found all the answers to my problems in regard to my family life and business. I saw with amazement the changes that happened when I followed the advice of the Bible.

I had not given much thought to the education of my children. Many times there was disharmony and strife which had negative results on our married life. As I read the Bible, I began to take my duties as the head of the family seriously. I prayed intensively for each member of my family and followed God's instructions for both my family and marriage. How wonderful to see love and harmony enter into our lives. You can really depend on the Word of God! The same was true for my business, the handling of money, and dealing with my customers.

More and more I began to trust the Word of God as I saw how my personal life came into order by obeying His Word. I read in the Bible about the gifts of the Holy Spirit and saw them begin to operate in and through my life. Again, I saw experientially that the Word of God is dependable and is true, and that the power of the Holy Spirit is mighty. As a new Christian, I did not know much about the arguments and doubts that some people have. I just believed. To me the Bible became a daily source of discovery, tried and tested in my own experience. Time and again I found out: It works!

Immediately after I had received the power of God through the baptism of the Holy Spirit, I began to stand up for Jesus and to testify. It had been thrilling

to see all of my twelve employees receive Jesus as
Lord within a week's time. We had a business totally
centered in Christ. Every morning we started
together with prayer and worship. It was so exciting
and I was on fire for the Lord.

One morning Lawrence, one of my employees,
walked into my office with a glass of water in which
he was putting an aspirin tablet. "What's wrong with
you? Do you have a headache? Let me pray for you.
The Lord will heal you!" I spoke boldly.

Astonished, he replied, "What?"

I just walked over to him, put my hands on him,
and said simply, "Oh, Jesus, I am just doing what You
say in the Bible to do. Trusting You, I put my hands
on him, You heal him!"

Lawrence did not need any aspirin. He dropped
the glass and shouted, "It's gone! It's gone!"

Laron studied medicine and worked part-time for
me. One Thursday afternoon he came into my office
on crutches, with a cast on his leg. He had a double
fracture that would not heal properly. So the doctors
decided to operate the next morning to pin the two
fractured pieces together.

"Laron," I said, "you know Jesus as your Lord
and Savior. He is also your physician. Has somebody
already prayed for you and laid hands on you?"

"Yes, I've had prayer," he replied, "but no one
has laid hands on me."

"Why don't we do it right now?" I put my hands
on his cast and in childlike faith I spoke a simple
prayer.

Suddenly he jumped up. "Did you hear it snap?

Did you hear it snap?"

No, I did not hear anything.

"I'm healed! I'm healed! I have no pain. Jesus healed me! I can take the cast off right now!" He rejoiced and danced through the room.

"No, no, no, don't do it!" I pleaded, fearful of such a drastic action. "Go to the hospital and let the doctors confirm it!"

The operation had been planned for six o'clock Friday morning. About ten o'clock I saw a car come speeding down the hill. It pulled into the gas station with brakes squealing. Laron jumped out of the car without a cast on his leg. He came running over, lifted me up, and danced around the gas pumps. "Jesus has healed me! Jesus has healed me!"

"What did the doctors say?" I asked curiously.

"Well, just before the scheduled operation they took another X-ray and handed it to the head surgeon. He took it into his hands and said, 'There is nothing wrong with that leg!'

"Then he himself took an X-ray. As he returned from the development room with yesterday's and today's films in his hand, he shook his head and questioned, 'What has happened to you?'

" 'I'm working for a funny kind of a boss,' I answered him, 'who believes that Jesus is alive and heals people. He prayed for me!'

"Still shaking his head, the doctor said, 'No one else could have done a better job!' "

At the end of my property was a huge billboard, 12 by 25 feet, which had been leased by my neighbor to an advertising company. Every car that pulled into my gas station saw this great big sign. One day a whiskey ad had been placed there, and this gave some of my customers a chance to make fun of me. They all knew that I confessed Jesus as my Lord. One fellow laughed at me and said, "You want to proclaim Jesus? Look what they have put up there. Next month they will probably put up a naked woman."

I really got angry. I called the company and asked them to take the whiskey ad down and put up something else. But they would not do it. Disappointed, I was sitting in my office and prayed, "Lord, You must do something! That billboard is spoiling our testimony!"

"No," the answer came back. "You do something. I have given you the 'rod of authority.' You have My word and My authority. In My name, use it!"

I walked out of my office, stood in front of the sign, pointed at it with my finger, and spoke out loud, "I command you in the name of Jesus to fall down!" Then I turned around and drove home.

As the morning attendant arrived the next day at the gas station, he phoned me immediately. "Steve, come over. The whole property is littered with paper. The whiskey ad has fallen down and all that is left is the white background. I don't know what has happened but the advertisement is strewn all over the ground!"

The company never again put up another advertisement like that as long as I was the owner of "Dippy Duck Car Wash." All future advertising was simply on products like candy or heating oil.

Thus, I learned to know the power of the Holy Spirit in a very practical way and to use the authority which we have in the name of Jesus. My personal training was to speak to the invisible world in agreement with the Word of God, and under the anointing of the Holy Spirit, so that God could manifest His results.

Time and time again, while I was traveling in the eastern block countries and challenging situations occurred, I remembered the scene of the whiskey sign. Then I dared to use "the rod of authority" in the name of Jesus.

I had read the verses in John 10 where four times Jesus said, "My sheep know My voice." John 18:37 says, "...*Every one who is of the truth hears My voice.*" When I read these, I said, "Wow! I know You Jesus. I'm born of the truth. But, I need to hear Your voice, Lord!" And so I said, "Oh, Lord, I want to hear Your voice! I want to hear Your voice! Speak to me!"

Even though He had spoken to me on several other occasions, it was something that seemed so rare. I wanted to have a daily fellowship and communion with Jesus so that I could hear His voice regularly.

Then one night--a cold night in February--Judy and I were sleeping as usual with the windows open. There was snow on the ground and it seemed almost colder inside the room than outside. At about 2:30 A.M., all of a sudden I was wide awake. This was very unusual for me. Normally, I can sleep through anything. I thought, "What in the world am I doing awake?" Then it dawned on me that maybe it was the

Lord's doing.

"Lord, did You wake me up?"

And that still inner voice spoke to me and said, "Yes, son."

That response was really something. I remember how there was such a settling of security in my heart when the Lord said "son." It established who He is and who I am. He's my Father and I'm His son.

"Oh, Lord, what do You want?" I said.

And the Lord spoke in a very clear voice in my heart and He said, "I want you to get out of bed. I want you to lie on the floor because I have something I want to tell you."

"Lord," I said, "I'll just lie right here in my nice warm bed and You can tell me what You want to tell me. It would be cold if I got out and laid on the floor."

"No," the Lord said. "I told you to get up, get out of bed, and lie down on the floor because I have something to tell you."

"Lord, no," I argued. "Tell me why. I want to stay here in this warm bed." This exchange went on several times.

The Lord got rather stern with me in His voice. Finally I said, "Okay, I'll do it." And so I got up out of bed and it was cold! The Lord had told me to lie at the foot of the bed, which was hardwood flooring. And I thought, "Oh, this is really going to be cold!" And when I went there and laid down, God had supernaturally heated that spot on the floor. It was as though I was lying on a beach in Hawaii. I was so thrilled!

If I hadn't been obedient and gotten up out of that

bed, I would have missed that experience.

I began to worship and praise the Lord. I lost track of time. Then I remembered. "Lord, You wanted to tell me something. What is it You wanted to tell me?"

"I wanted to tell you that you could get up and go back to bed."

"What?" I was shocked.

"Yes, you can get up and get into bed."

"I don't understand," I complained. "You tell me to get out of bed. I get out. You said to lie down at the foot of the bed. I laid down here. And now You tell me the thing You wanted to tell me was that I could go back and get in bed?"

"Yes," He said. "I wanted to see if you would obey Me. It's not just good enough to hear My voice. I wanted to see if you would obey me in something small."

The Lord taught me that if I would be obedient to His voice in the little things, then He would begin to give me other more important opportunities. I didn't realize that there would be a time coming in my life when that same voice that tested me and taught me that night would be the one that would speak to me when I was ministering behind the Iron Curtain and say, "Don't go to that place," and it would save my life.

One day, while Judy and I were driving in downtown Seattle, we were watching a group of young people putting up a sign promoting homosexuality. It was shocking. So, I commanded the evil spirit behind that sinfulness to be bound. God, however, pointed out to me, "You have a sign, use it for Me!"

"Yes, surely I do have that 37-foot-high three-dimensional sign on the revolving post with the duck on top of it." The next morning I woke up at 5:30 A.M. and had the impression to place these words on the sign: "If you love Jesus, tell somebody today!"

I did not feel at ease on my way to work. Should I really do it? You just don't do things like that! You just don't mix religion with business. But I wanted to learn to hear the voice of the Lord and I knew that I could only achieve that if I would be willing to do what He was saying. With shaky hands, I placed each letter on the sign.

The first customer came at seven o'clock. While I was filling his tank, I saw that he was crying. "Who put up that sign?" he inquired.

"I, ah, I did." I was stammering.

"How did you know that those were the last words my mother told me on her deathbed eight and a half years ago?" he said sobbing. He began to tell me how he grew up in a Christian home and his mother had always repeated that it was not enough just to believe in your heart. "You must confess publicly," she had said again and again. He had never dared to do it. Therefore, on her deathbed she whispered these last words, "If you love Jesus, tell somebody today!" And, then she died.

I was deeply moved by the effect of the words I had placed on the sign that morning. So, I asked the man, "Will you do it today? Will you invite Jesus into your life?" He stretched his hand out of the window.

With my oily hands, I grabbed his and, right at the gas pump, we experienced that holy moment as Jesus entered this man's life.

After that incident, I said, "Lord, whatever You want up on that sign, I will put it up there!"

From that day on, every morning before work, I got a sentence from Jesus that I placed on the sign. This went on for over a year until I gave up the business and went to Europe.

The short messages on the sign spoke to the hearts of the people passing by: a Bible verse, a word of knowledge, or an encouraging saying. Our gas station was right next to a very busy highway with about 43,000 cars going by each day. At first I had been afraid the sign might drive customers away, but it was not so at all. They did not turn away, but rather business increased.

Soon we saw the good results. Some customers came in just out of curiosity and we gave them our testimony. Others came with personal needs and we could pray for them. Customers gave their lives to Jesus, were filled with the Holy Spirit, and received healing. Soon we had so many people inquiring that I brought in a 20-foot travel trailer and put it behind the car wash and used it as a chapel.

The newspapers picked up the story about the "crazy" gas station. One Saturday a pastor called saying, "I need a fresh word for my Sunday sermon. What do you have on your sign today?" That is how he got the inspiration for his message.

My employees and I found ourselves on an exciting mission field. At least once a day, the Lord gave us a special word for individual customers. I did not find it all as easy as some may think. There I was, filling up a gas tank, and Jesus spoke to my heart, "My son, speak to the man concerning his problem!" Then He showed me the area of concern.

"But, Jesus, that's my customer. I can't tell him that. I would drive him away."

Regardless of my reservations, I knew one thing. If I wanted to improve in knowing the voice of the Lord, I had to be willing to be obedient. So, I talked to the customer. At first he was stunned, but it was true and I was able to help. He left a grateful customer.

There had been times in the past when I was so zealous and aggressive in my testimony that I drove people away. In my ambitious way I would try to ram the love of God down a person's throat even if it killed him.

But I learned how important it is to have the leading of the Holy Spirit. If it is the Lord giving the direction to move and your heart is filled with love for the other person, there will be good fruit.

Some businessmen came by to invite me for a cup of coffee. As always they asked the question, "Tell me, how did you become so bold in witnessing for Jesus?"

"At first I thought you were ridiculous," one of them said, "but now I can see the results and your business is not suffering. I also believe in Jesus, but I don't have the courage to do anything like that."

After that, it was my turn to share how Jesus came into my life, and how the power of the Holy Spirit had changed me. Now I had only one desire: to feed on His Word, to have His power within me, and to be led by His voice.

This period of my life was a time of intensive training, learning to listen to God's voice. At that time, I did not comprehend the prophetic significance but, as I began to travel, the same voice spoke again and again to me and He was able to warn me or lead me on the correct route. The school of listening to the voice of Jesus later on saved my life more than once.

CHAPTER 4

LEAVE EVERTHING...FOLLOW ME!

After a time I sensed that there would be more important things to do in my life. Without being able to explain it specifically I knew somehow that my time at the gas pumps at "Dippy Duck Car Wash" had been a training period to prepare me for greater things in life. That was the time for me to learn to be faithful and obedient in the small things which God had put before me so He could someday entrust me with the greater things.

One morning in September of 1972, before opening the station, I was sitting in my office praying. The Lord began to speak very clearly to my heart, "My son, the day will come that you will get up, leave this office and never return."

I wondered, "How can this be possible?" We had put all our savings in this new project. We had not only sold our restaurant and our house, we even took out a bank loan to finance the rest. How could it be possible to leave everything? I also knew that these thoughts would be very difficult to handle for my dear wife, Judy. She grew up with the idea that material security is the most important thing in life, she valued a nice home and a good savings account. The Lord had gotten me to the point where I was willing to do anything for Him, because I had experienced so many wonderful things with Him. I wondered about Judy, how would He crack that nutshell? So I prayed, "Lord, if this is what You have in mind, then You have to make this clear to Judy!"

Interestingly, Jesus talked to Judy the same day. While she had been doing her housework and thought about the increasingly exciting life in Jesus, the Lord began to talk to her and she said in her heart, "Jesus, whatever You want from us, I am ready to follow You!" When I came home that night and she began to share her thoughts with me, I saw with great surprise how the Lord had already moved in her heart. She told me that no matter what the Lord tells us to do, we must do it. So I was able to tell her what the Lord had shown me during my prayer time before work. My assurance increased that it was God speaking and not my imagination.

The Lord began to prepare us with many small signs through His Word for that day when we would leave everything behind and begin a new style of living.

During all this time there was one Bible text that kept coming to my mind. In Luke 5:1-11 Jesus called

Peter and two more men to be His disciples. Just at the time when Peter was having a great catch of fish, Jesus told him, *"Do not fear, from now on you will be catching men."* The next verse reads, *"And when they had brought their boats to land, they left everything and followed Him."*

As I was reading these verses, I asked myself, "Who took care of the fish? After such a big catch, someone had to carry on the business, to look after the ships and sell the fish." In my business, after three years, we had finally begun to make a profit. This was "fish on the beach." It was just at the height of his business career that the Lord spoke to Peter, "Follow after Me!" For Peter, the Lord was more important than anything else. He left everything and followed Him.

The time was 5:30 on a Wednesday afternoon in February 1973. I was putting all business papers in order so I could lock my office. The Lord spoke to me, "My son, today is the day. Get up, walk out of the office, and never return!"

Hearing His voice speaking so clearly to my heart did not frighten me at all. I was prepared and actually had been waiting for that moment. Now the time was right; a new way of living could begin. I got up from my desk and walked over to the safe where I had about $14,000. I stretched out my hands to reach for it, but I pulled them back. "My son, that does not belong to you!" I attempted to take my checkbook. "It is not yours anymore!"

"How shall we keep on going?" came to my mind like a bolt of lightning. Then it appeared to me clearly that I was no longer the steward of this business. A totally new way of life was beginning. I walked out, locked the door, and since that moment have never been back in that office again. At that time I did not see the prophetic significance of leaving all of this suddenly behind. There was a time when the children of Israel had to leave Egypt suddenly and move on. There is coming a point in history when they will face a situation like that once again.

I too have experienced what it means to suddenly leave everything and to follow Jesus, and Him alone.

When I went home, told Judy all about it, and was waiting for the evening meal, the devil began to work on my mind, "Now, who will open up the business in the morning? Who will pay all the employees on Friday? Who will pay all the bills at the end of the month?"

I could not find any peace as these thoughts came. Am I crazy? Did the Lord really speak or am I out of my mind? We sat down with the children to dinner and I just could not eat. My stomach was churning. Did I really do the right thing? How will it all come out?

In these critical moments Judy was very perceptive and understanding. She did not ask any questions, or bother me with doubts, and I noticed that she sensed what I was feeling and stood by my side during the inner battle. In these moments, while I was hardly able to manage my own thoughts, the phone rang. The male voice on the other end of the line sounded very excited, "Steve, God just spoke to me!"

"Wonderful, Bob," I said, recognizing his voice.

"I know how that feels."

"Really? He told me something almost unbelievable. I don't know whether I should believe it. I don't know if I dare say it."

"Well, what is it?" I questioned, burning with curiosity.

He began stammering and then spilled it out. "The Lord told me to come to you and take over Dippy Duck Car Wash."

This man did not have the slightest idea about the things we had been battling with. We had never talked to anyone about it so no one would think we were out of our minds. Exactly at the moment of our greatest testing, Bob called. I knew the Lord had sent him to show me I was hearing clearly from Him.

"Bob," I said enthusiastically, "when can you come to pick up the keys, receipts, and paperwork?" He was indeed surprised. I began to share all of what had happened and he clearly understood that he was the answer to our prayers.

"I won't be able to make it today," he explained, "but how about six o'clock in the morning? Can I pick up everything at that time?" That was all right with me.

At six o'clock the next morning, I handed him the keys, the combination to the safe, and everything else pertaining to the business.

He took over the money and the bills of the business. Since that day, I have never returned to the office or had anything to do with the business. I had been pondering the contents of Luke 5:1-11 for months. It became a reality to the letter, "...*they left everything and followed Him!"*

For Judy and for me, this step was the beginning of a new walk with the Lord. We began to seek His face as much as we knew how and He continued to guide us. Despite the fact that our experiences had been like a movie, and some people might have envied us, it was not always easy to walk in this new path.

We made many mistakes, but God was always present to lead us back on the new pathway, just as it says in Psalm 37:23,24, *"The steps of a man are established by the Lord; and He delights in his way. When he falls, he shall not be hurled headlong; because the Lord is the One who holds his hand."* That's the way it worked with us. The Lord established our steps and as we fell, He picked us up again.

It was at the end of a meeting of the Full Gospel Business Men that the speaker, Don Ostrom, made this call, "Is there someone here who feels the calling of God on his life and wants to make himself available? Are you ready to be an instrument in God's hand and be sent even to other nations to share your life with others?"

"Oh yes, Lord," I replied in my heart, "that would be wonderful. All those things that I have experienced with You, I would love to share them with the people in other countries. But I have no business, and no money, there is no possibility for me to go."

Again, I heard the call from the front, "Regardless of time or money, if you have a willing heart, God will make it all possible." Don asked for those willing to come to the front. Suddenly, I stood up and went forward and believed God, that He could send me.

Shortly after this meeting, one of the members of
the Full Gospel Business Men's Fellowship, John Andor, who had moved to Braunschweig, West Germany
three months earlier on business, called Fred
Doerflein in Seattle, "Please come with a group of
businessmen and help me. God has opened doors and
the people would like to hear more about Jesus and
the full Gospel!"

When I heard about the request, it was a clear
leading in my heart, "This is from God!" Even though
I did not have any money, God provided the means.
So in April of 1973 I traveled with a group of ten
businessmen to Europe for four weeks of ministry.
We traveled through many cities and saw tremendous
things happen as people gave their lives to Jesus.
They were filled with the Holy Spirit and many
received physical healings. We went about our
ministry with great excitement and enthusiasm. Only
later did we realize that we had shocked people with
our bold ways of doing things. The blessings remained
anyway. It was interesting to watch how God could do
so many good things in spite of our mistakes.

During all this traveling, there was something
wrong in my heart concerning my relationship to the
German people. The Lord had to work on it.

In order to see something of the beauty of Germany, we went sightseeing on the Rhine River
downstream from Bingen to Koblenz. This was my
first trip to Europe and I was impressed with the for-
tresses and castles along the hills by the river.

I also watched the vineyards with great amazement. It was April and the vines had been pruned so far down that you could hardly imagine how life could come out of them. They were all low stumps with almost no branches. "What a miracle," I thought to myself, "that from these drastically pruned vines, branches will grow out and in the fall they will bear wonderful fruit. What a significant amount of growth in such a short period of time."

That's when the Holy Spirit began to speak to my heart, "By the time you leave this boat, you will be as small as one of these pruned vines." Immediately I realized what that meant. Cleansing, purging, cutting. In front of my eyes I saw the words of Jesus in John 15. He is the vine, we are the branches. He wants to cleanse and to cut, so that we will bear much more fruit.

As I was standing at the rear of the boat gazing at the countryside, a dialogue began in my heart, "What is the real reason you are in Germany?"

"Lord, You know why I am here. I am here to share and to proclaim the Gospel!"

A short pause, "My son, what is the real reason in your heart that you are here?"

"Lord, You know I am here to proclaim Your deeds and heal the sick!"

Another pause and then again, "My son, what is the real motive of your heart?"

Without thinking, it burst out of me, "I am here to show those Jew killers how to love in the name of Jesus!"

I could not believe that these kinds of thoughts were still in my heart. The countryside around me

suddenly looked blurry as tears came into my eyes.
"Oh, Lord, I did not know that this hatred was still in
my heart. Jesus, please forgive me and cleanse me!"

Jesus then told me, "Look at all the things that
have happened on this trip even though you had the
wrong motives in your heart. The people gave their
lives to Me, they were filled with the Holy Spirit, and
they received healing. Now, I want to show you all the
things that will happen with the right motives in your
heart when My love guides you to reach the hearts of
the people."

In these minutes God changed my heart toward
the German people. The wounds of my Jewish past
were healed, I was able to forgive, and as I walked off
the boat, I was not the same anymore.

Our last days in Europe were spent in
Braunschweig at a place that I had feared the most. It
was the last place I wanted to stay. We were given
quarters in a house called the "Kaffeestube,"a Christian rehabilitation center for alcoholics and drug addicts. I had no sympathy for people with long hair.
They all looked wild to me, and I had never had
anything to do with alcoholics and drug addicts. I did
not want to have anything to do with them and did not
know how to help them.

To my surprise, I had no fear of them. I began to
love them and they loved me too. With some of them I
was able to talk and pray, and I saw their deliverance
from addiction through the love of Jesus. Suddenly, I
realized that the attitude of my heart had changed. It
is amazing to see what can happen if we allow the love
of Jesus in us to flow to others. No matter what a per-

son has done, whether he is young or old, whatever
sin besets him or how he looks, Jesus loves him. Jesus
taught me to see the people around me with His eyes.
He opened my heart toward them, and it was not my
love, but His love that was able to spark others.

The last night before our departure we met once
again in Braunschweig, just to say goodbye. During
our time of prayer, God spoke through prophecy that
one of the Americans would return to Braunschweig
to live there. We looked at each other, smiled and
joked, "That must be you!" We teased one another
because nobody seriously thought he might be the
one. We went to bed and the next morning all my
beloved new friends sang a farewell song to us as we
stood in front of the house. As we were riding in the
car on our way to the airport, tears came into my eyes
and I began to cry. It was a cry from the depth of my
heart. I tried to control it, but could not stop the
tears.

On the flight home to Seattle I found that
everytime my good friend Fred Doerflein tried to talk
with me I just sobbed and cried and had no explana-
tion for it.

At home I had many things to share with Judy. As
I finished telling her everything, I had a clear
thought, "Maybe that prophecy had been for me?"
We fasted together for seven days to seek the mind of
the Lord to see if we were supposed to return to Germany. After the fast, it was clear to us. Germany
would be our next place of ministry! In a very short
time we had cleared our household and put the fur-
niture in storage. This was not difficult for us to do

since we had already given up many things.

We booked the tickets for our daughters, Lynn and Michele, and us to depart in June of 1973. As the day of departure arrived and I was to pick up the tickets, I did not have enough money to pay for them. Hesitantly, I left the house to go to the travel agency. I was $370 short. I wondered how in the world I would pay for those tickets. I felt led to stop at a restaurant for a cup of coffee and a man who owed me $320 was there. When he saw me, he came right over to me.

"Steve, am I ever glad to see you!" he said. "I've been wondering how to get ahold of you. I didn't know where you had moved to. I've been wanting to return this money to you." And he handed me the $320.

Then I went to the shopping mall where the travel agency was located. Since I still was $50 short for the tickets, I made a detour through a Christian book store to kill time. Once inside I saw a lady I had met one time before.

"Steve, where have you been? I've been expecting you. I was praying this morning and the Lord told me that I was to give you something and that I would run into you. I've been wondering all day where and when I'd see you. It's so late in the afternoon that I wondered if I'd missed you."

She handed me an envelope and when I opened it, there was a fifty dollar bill. When I walked into the travel agency to pick up the tickets for the evening departure, I had exactly the amount of money necessary to pay for the tickets.

With joy we left for the airport having those tickets in our hands. Between us Judy and I had one dollar and twenty-eight cents. Equipped with that meager amount, we were on our way to go to a country where we did not know the language or what to expect. The only thing we knew was that somebody would meet us at the airport in Hanover. We really had to trust the Lord to take care of everything. Naturally, many of our friends were at Sea-Tac Airport to see us off. As we came to the security gate, my father squeezed an envelope into my hands and said, "This is a letter, open it later on the plane."

Halfway to London I remembered that envelope. I opened it and found 2,500 German marks ($1,000) inside. It was an overwhelming sign of the care and presence of our God. We had obeyed and He had cared for us.

CHAPTER 5

GOD SENDS AN ANGEL

There came a time in my life when I recognized that there were certain things in me that needed to be changed--things I could not seem to change in my own strength. I had really been crying out as David did, *"Search me, O God, and know my heart; Try me and know my anxious thoughts; And see if there be any hurtful way in me, And lead me in the everlasting way"* (Psalms 139:23-24). I continued crying out to God, asking Him to search my heart.

We were living back in the United States temporarily but I knew the Lord was telling me I had to go to Amsterdam and make two telephone calls. I really thought that was odd but I told Judy, "I have to go to Amsterdam and make two phone calls."

"It would be a whole lot cheaper to call them from Seattle," she said, "than to fly all the way over there to do it." But Judy was learning, too, that when the Lord says to do something, you do it whether it seems logical or not. She agreed that I should go. It was August, 1974.

One man I knew I was to call was John Andor. I knew him very well. I had known him when we lived in Seattle and then we became even closer friends while we were living in Braunschweig, where John had also moved. And the other man, Henk Paulson, I had met and talked with for only about twenty minutes one day several months before in the United States. He lived in Holland and had said, "If you ever get to Holland, give me a call and come and see me." Now people do that, but you usually don't know if they really mean it! But in this case I knew the Lord was saying to call him.

So I flew to Amsterdam. There were certain things I knew in my heart that God said I was going to do. One I just kept buried in my heart. God had told me to begin to travel behind the Iron Curtain in eastern Europe. I didn't know how I would be able to do this. I didn't have a car in Europe. I didn't have any contacts. I didn't know anything. I didn't know anybody. I only knew that I must go.

When I arrived in Amsterdam, the first call I made was to Germany to contact John. His wife, Benta, answered the phone. "Steve," she said, "where are you?"

"I'm in Amsterdam," I replied.

"Oh," she said, "John is not here. He's in Holland, and he'll be staying not far from where you are tonight. I'll give you his number."

So I called John and he was delighted that I was there. He asked me to come to the house where he was staying. They were going to have a meeting about forming a chapter of the Full Gospel Business Men in that community.

Then I called the other man whom I had only met briefly. "Steve!" He said, "How good of you to call." I was surprised that he remembered me. "Can you come here tomorrow?" he asked.

"Yes, that would be possible," I told him.

"If you catch the train from where you are, you will be here at exactly 2:20 P.M. I'll meet you and we'll have some time to fellowship together." And so it was arranged.

That night I went to the meeting where John was. I had a brief time with John after the meeting was over, but then he had to go back to Germany that evening. The people invited me to stay overnight.

I went to bed, turned the light out, and was lying in bed when all of a sudden I knew there was an angel standing right there in the room. The presence of the angel was so strong, so real! I knew exactly where he was standing. So I looked over real quickly, thinking I certainly would see an angel with a flaming sword standing in the corner. I couldn't see a thing. It was just pitch black.

So I got up and turned the light on but I still couldn't see him. Yet I knew he was there. So I just turned the light off and said, "Well, Lord, I know there is an angel standing there. I can't see him, but I would like to see an angel." Then I put the thought out of my mind and went to sleep.

The next morning after breakfast with the family, my host, Peter, took me to the train station. It was just a small station in a little community outside of Utrecht, Holland.

"Look, I'll buy your ticket," he said. "You don't speak Dutch so I'll buy it for you." So he went over to the place to buy the ticket and I noticed there was no one else around. We were the only two people on the whole platform. He bought the ticket and handed it to me.

"Okay, here's your ticket. Now you'll catch the train to Rotterdam and change your train there to go south to the city of Roosendaal."

"Okay," I said. "Thank you!"

"I'll see you," he said as he waved his hand. "Goodbye." And he left.

I picked up my two bags and I walked over to the track where the train was going to come. Now, I had ridden many trains in Europe up to that time. I had learned well that when you ride a train, you must be sure to get on the car that is going to the city that you are going to. The train may be scheduled to go to several cities in a certain direction and then it will stop while some cars are disconnected and sent off to the other specified cities. So you must get on the right car. And I knew that.

When the train came, I noticed the first car said "Rotterdam," the second car said "Rotterdam," and the third and fourth cars said "Rotterdam." There were only five cars on the train. I didn't bother to look to see where the fifth car of the train was going. I just assumed that since the first four cars were going to Rotterdam, the fifth car must be going to Rotterdam too. And the train stopped with the door of the fifth car exactly in front of me. When it went by, where I would normally have been able to see the name on the car, I had reached down to pick up my bags and I just didn't see it.

So I got in the car and the train took off. About forty-five minutes and three towns later, we stopped at a particular station. I was just kind of passing the time away when the door opened. A man stepped into the car, and in perfect English he said, "Excuse me, sir, but you are on the wrong car to go to Rotterdam to change your train so you can get to Roosendaal. Would you follow me, please?" And he stepped off the train.

I sat there and thought, "How did he know to speak to me in English? How did he know where I was going?" And so I grabbed my two bags and I jumped off the car to follow him. And as I got off that car, I saw that it was being disconnected right there. I looked and saw that the sign said "The Hague," the capital city of the Netherlands. The train was splitting and that car was going off to The Hague, which was in the opposite direction of where I wanted to go- to Rotterdam-to change trains.

So I ran and I caught up with the man. I was within six feet of him and looked him straight in his eyes and said, "Don't you go away. I have some questions I want to ask you." I turned to set my bags down. I turned back a moment later and there was no one standing there. Absolutely no one.

I couldn't understand what had happened. "What's going on? Where is he?" I said. And so I looked under the train, I ran up ahead of the train, I looked all over. I could not find that man anywhere. He had vanished. Gone! And then all of a sudden the still voice of the Holy Spirit said, "But, son, you asked Me last night to let you see an angel."

"God, this is not even a spiritual situation!" I said, feeling rather puzzled. "Why would You have to send an angel to get me on the right car? So what if I went to The Hague? I could have just turned right around and caught another train back. It would have been only an hour's difference."

I picked up my bags and got on the right car. I sat down in the compartment and rejoiced. I was ecstatic because of the experience. Then all of a sudden a sobering thought rose up within me and I stopped. "Wait a minute, Lord," I said. "I am not satisfied with seeing an angel. I want to see You." And there was something in that experience--that answer to prayer--that made me recognize that it might also be possible to see the Lord.

Exodus 33 came to my mind where Moses stood face to face with the Lord, and the Lord spoke with Moses as a man speaks with a friend. I remembered in Genesis 12 where the Lord appeared to Abraham. And I also thought how Jesus had said, "I only do what I see My Father in heaven do." And Paul had said that he was taken up into heaven and things happened there that he couldn't describe or speak about. "Lord," I said boldly, "that's the kind of experience that I want to have now."

I made my connection in Rotterdam to go to Roosendaal. I stepped off the train and my friend Henk was all excited. "Thank God you were on this train!" he exclaimed. "My plans have changed since I talked to you last night. I did not know how to get hold of you. If you had missed this train, we would have missed each other. In twenty minutes I have to leave Holland. Some things have come up and I must go. I would not have been here to meet you if you had been late."

"Oh, really?" I said, pondering the events on the train.

I got into Henk's Volkswagen Camper Bus. "Steven," he said, "last night, when I hung up the phone after talking to you, God told me that I'm to give you this camper bus and furnish you with names and addresses of people in eastern Europe. You're supposed to go there and minister to your brothers in Christ."

I was flabbergasted. Then I found out what he did. He was the Eastern European Director for Open Doors, the organization that is headed by Brother Andrew. He was also head of another group called the Eastern European Bible Mission.

If I had not been on the right train, the whole opportunity for ministry in eastern Europe and Russia would never have happened at that time. But it was in God's perfect timing. He saw to it that it happened. I am fully confident in my heart that it was an angel that God sent to get me on the right train car so I'd be there at exactly the right time.

CHAPTER 6

GOD SPEAKS THROUGH VISIONS

Henk Paulson left his apartment and his camper bus for me to use. Then he took off on special business behind the Iron Curtain.

Before I had left Seattle, I had called Phil Israelson. I told Phil that I was going to Holland and he had said that he was going there too. It turned out that he was staying only fifteen kilometers from Henk's house. I went over and got Phil and brought him back with me, and we had a really significant time in prayer. Some things happened there spiritually that were another step of preparation in God's plan to answer the cry of my heart. Paul said in Galatians 2:20, *"I have been crucified with Christ; and it is no longer I who live."* I really wanted to know, not only by faith in the Word of God, but by experience, what it meant to be crucified with Christ.

Phil and I drove over to Germany and I dropped him off in Hanover to visit a friend. Then I continued on to Braunschweig, which is only another forty-five kilometers away. And I went to the Kaffeestube, the Teen Challenge type of house that helps drug addicts and alcoholics--where Judy and I had lived when we moved to Braunschweig in 1973. They have a little room for guests, like a prophet's chamber, up on the fourth floor of their building.

I arranged for the room.

I told the people at Kaffeestube what I was going to be doing in the room. "Don't bother me," I warned them. "Don't even call me. I don't know how long I am going to be here but just leave me alone." They knew me and knew that I meant what I said. So, they left me alone.

I went into the room and said, "Lord, either I am going to die in this room or You are going to change my life. I'm not coming out of here until one or the other happens." I was very serious with God. I would fast, and pray, and read the Bible until God did something to change my heart. I knew that God was leading me this way. I knew there were things in me I couldn't deal with. There was no way in my own strength that I could deal with pride, jealousy, bitterness, hate, envy, and strife, and other things that should not be there. And the number one thing was really pride. I just couldn't get rid of it. So I asked the Lord to do something.

While I was sitting in a chair, the power of God came into the room and I knew I had to get out of the chair and lie on the floor. The power was so great I couldn't get up. And I stayed there six and a half days. Things began to happen to me spiritually of such a deep nature that I wondered what was going on. For the first time in my life, I had such an intimate and personal time with Jesus, that I could say with Paul, *"I...heard inexpressible words, which a man is not permitted to speak"* (II Corinthians 12:4).

I really wondered if I was still in my own right mind. But God in His mercy sent a man to see me. This man opened the door where I was and the power of God hit him. He fell on his face and said, "I can't breathe in here." And he crawled out and closed the door. He couldn't stay with me in God's power but just a few minutes.

About a day and a half later another man came to visit me. He opened the door and the power of the Lord hit him and he fell down. He crawled into the room and he stayed with me about twenty minutes. And that was all he could take. He couldn't stand any more. It was impossible to even stand up in this room. The glory and the power and the weight that come with the manifested glory of God that was in that room just pushed people down. No one could stand up. And, finally, he crawled out and closed the door.

God sent those two people to me to show me that what was happening was actually something very real and spiritual, and that I wasn't losing my mind.

During these days, the Lord was taking me mainly through the book of Isaiah. This was where I was reading almost constantly for the six and a half days. The Lord would make everything so real to me. It was an ongoing process of revelation.

After the second person had left, something

began to happen that was so supernatural that it may be hard for some to believe. But all of a sudden just like that night that I had experienced an angel's presence in that house back in Holland, I knew there was an angelic being standing in the room with me there. In fact I knew that there were two standing in the room with me and I knew I was going to see them.

I turned to look where the first one was, and it was the most awe-inspiring thing I had ever seen in my life! He was very, very large. The room had a high ceiling--probably a good twenty feet--and the belt buckle of this creature was about twenty-five feet high. He was a creature of God and he stood higher than the roof of the house.

I don't even know how to put this into words, but he was not limited by the physical dimensions of the house or this world. And I looked over to the other spot where I knew there was another one, and sure enough, there he was! Two of them--of these angelic creatures--were standing there.

I can't even adequately describe them to you. All I can say is that after I read Revelation 4:6-9 and the tenth chapter of Ezekiel, and Genesis 3:24 and saw how the writers tried to describe what they were seeing, I understood how it's just about impossible.

They never spoke to me. They never said a word. I didn't talk to them. But I knew that God had put them there for my protection.

They each had three pairs of wings. They stood absolutely motionless and yet they knew everything and could see everything that was going on all around -in every direction, up, down, around, everywhere

-just like it says in the Bible.

Then the Lord sent one more person to me, my dear friend, Phil Israelson. He came on over from Hanover, where I had dropped him off. When he opened the door, the power of God hit him. He fell on the floor and as he did he said, "Steve, what's going on here?" And all of a sudden he looked over towards this one place in the room and by the look on his face, I knew he had seen one of the angelic creatures.

"Oh, Lord, thank you," I said gratefully under my breath. "You've sent somebody to see them too so that I'll know I'm not having a hallucination or something."

"Phil," I said, "do you see anything else?" And he looked exactly at the place where the other one was and I said, "Phil, I want you to describe to me what you see. I've got to know whether you are seeing-that we are seeing the same thing." And he began to describe them, and I said, "That's it!" And he described to me exactly what I had seen, to the smallest details.

We continued to read in the book of Isaiah the whole time that Phil was there with me. He would read aloud and I would say, "Phil, do you know what that means?" And the Lord would give me the revelation, the illumination of that word. Oh, what a time we had! Phil stayed with me for two and a half days and then he had to leave.

After he left, I was there still on the floor with my eyes closed and my head down. Suddenly, Jesus was right there with me. And He spoke to me. Was it an audible voice? Did I hear it inside myself? I really

can't say for sure. All I know is that it was so plain
and so clear.

"I want you to trust Me," He said.

"Lord, I trust You," I said.

"I want you to trust Me," He said again.

"Lord, I trust You," I said.

"You have to trust Me!" He said a third time, emphatically.

"Lord, I trust You," I cried out. From the depths
of my being I was telling Jesus that I trusted Him.

I opened my eyes, and Jesus was standing right in
front of me. He was just standing there, and the only
thing I can say is that it was as though He had an axe
in His hand. And then I saw something that was the
most horrible, ugly thing I've ever seen in my life.
And I screamed because it was so terrible. I'd never
seen anything like it. And I screamed out, "Lord,
what is that?"

And Jesus said, "That's your heart."

"God, I can't stand it!" I said.

"I can't stand it either," Jesus said. And He took
an axe and He laid it to my heart and He said, "This is
your pride!" He laid that axe right to the root of that
pride that was in me. And my old self literally died in
that room. I knew experientially the meaning of Matthew 3:10: *"And the axe is already laid at the root of
the trees; every tree therefore that does not bear good
fruit is cut down and thrown into the fire."*

Now, I already knew Jesus as my Messiah. I
already knew that His blood had cleansed me of my
sin. I knew Him as my baptizer in the Holy Spirit. I
knew Him as my healer. I knew Him as Lord. I knew

Jesus in all these things. But I didn't know Him in His crucifixion in a way that I had to know, so that I could really be raised from the dead in the power of His resurrection and live with Him.

When this happened, I screamed, and if anyone had been anywhere near there, I know they would have thought I was being murdered. But they were down in the basement, five floors down, eating their afternoon meal. Then Jesus began to go through the other things that were in my heart: jealousy, envy, strife, hatred, and bitterness--just roots! They weren't things manifesting themselves in my life, but the roots of those things were there, and needed to be taken away. And each time He did it, I experienced spiritual pain with physical effects--I can't adequately explain it--except that I believe that I physically died in that room and was resurrected. Jesus resurrected me! When it was over, I can say that I have never ever felt so clean and pure as at that time.

And then Jesus said, "Don't let a seed of any of these things enter back into your heart lest they turn into a root and become a tree and bear forth branches and bring forth evil fruit." The warning was scriptural. (Hebrews 12:15: *"See to it that no one comes short of the grace of God; that no root of bitterness springing up causes trouble, and by it many be defiled."*) It was something that I will never forget.

During this time Jesus also led me in a vision into a hospital room in which a girl with a white nightgown was lying. Jesus walked over to her and with a certain gesture laid His hands on her. Then He told me, "When you see this scene again, then do exactly the same as you have seen Me do!"

And then I was able to get up. I sat in a large overstuffed chair, just quietly worshipping the Lord from the depth of my heart-a depth that I had never known before of worship and praise. And that's when I had the vision. It was as though it was projected on a large screen. I saw a lot of people and I recognized that they were Jewish faces. And there were so many! Then from a particular viewpoint, I could see that there was a multitude of Jewish people--hundreds and hundreds of thousands of them.

Then my angle of vision changed again. This time I saw it from a height that enabled me to see the nation they were in. It was the Soviet Union, and these were Jewish people that were being gathered from different parts of that nation. On many small streets they were gathering from various regions of Russia. They were coming together and began to walk upon a big super highway that God had built that was bound westward. Somehow I knew that this was a highway that only certain people could walk on. Only those that God permitted could get on it. And as they walked, they began to come forth out of the USSR.

At the same time there were ministries that God raised up that were as great as or even greater than that of Moses in Egypt. And they began to proclaim unto the Soviet authorities, "Thus saith the Lord God of Israel, let My people go!" And the Soviets refused. Then God, through these ministries, brought great judgment upon the Soviet Union. The catastrophies were so severe that the whole nation was brought to its knees. Then it was as though the Soviet Union coughed up the Jewish people and they began to walk on this specially-built highway.

As I watched, I saw that the highway continued on through Poland, through Warsaw. It continued on through East Germany, through the city of Berlin. From Berlin it crossed over the border into West Germany at Helmstadt into the city of Braunschweig. This highway that had been built by God continued on to the city of Hanover and then into Holland, and it came up into the northern parts of Holland where the Jewish people got on ships and went to Israel.

All along the way I saw people laying hands upon the Jews who were sick and they were healed. The people offered the food they had, which was not enough to feed all the Jewish refugees. But when the people offered it to the Lord, it was expanded to feed the multitude-just like when Jesus fed the five thousand. It was awesome!

I was completely overwhelmed with the things I had seen. What should I do with it? If I was supposed to share this with others, I needed confirmation from the Lord, to know for sure that it was not my own imagination.

"Jesus," I said, "this is wonderful, but what do You want me to do with it?"

"Share it next Monday night at the prayer meeting," He said.

"Jesus," I prayed, "I need to have confirmation out of the Word of God and through a miracle. Otherwise I cannot share this vision. I must know that this is from You before I can talk about it."

The Lord showed me the verses in the prophetic

books of the Bible where He says that He will lead His
people out of the country of the north. The biblical
witness of the coming of the Jews out of Russia is unmistakably clear and rooted in the prophecies of the
Old Testament. It really lifted the burden from me to
know that this, which I had seen, has already been the
message of the Old Testament.

And as I was still sitting there pondering these
things, I was interrupted by a knock on the door. Jutta, the wife of one of the leaders at the house, asked
me to go with her to a hospital to pray for a girl in the
psychiatric ward. The mother of the girl had called
and explained that her daughter had tried to commit
suicide so it had been necessary to commit her. She
was heavily sedated on drugs.

Her mother felt the doctors weren't really helping her, for she just wasn't getting any better. The
mother had remembered that once in a while her
daughter had come to the meetings at the Kaffeestube and was always so peaceful after being at
these meetings. So she had called and asked if some of
us could go and see her.

My time alone with Jesus had seemed to come to
an end, I felt, so I was willing to go.

At first the doctors resisted letting us in, but
finally gave us permission to go in for just ten
minutes.

Jutta entered first and I followed. I could not
believe my eyes! This was the same scene I had seen
in the vision, the exact hospital room with one bed
and a girl in a white nightgown. Had not Jesus told
me, "When you see that scene again, do exactly as

you have seen Me do!" Suddenly, the verse out of John 5:19 came into my mind, *"Truly, truly, I say to you, the Son can do nothing of Himself, unless it is something He sees the Father doing; for whatever the Father does, these things the Son also does in like manner."*

There was not the slightest doubt in my mind as I walked over to the girl, who was lying lifelessly on her bed under heavy sedation. As I had seen in the vision, I laid my hands on her and prayed. I was only a servant of the Lord, but I knew that I was speaking His words, and Jesus touched her. Immediately, she sat upright on her bed and was out of the fog the medication had caused. I looked at her and said, "I will see you again in thirty days."

I did not know why I had said this, but one month later a young lady came to the front with her parents during a meeting at Braunschweig. All three gave their lives to Jesus. At first I had not noticed who they were until the girl said, "Don't you know me? Thirty days ago you prayed for me. Only a few hours later the doctors released me, completely healed!"

After I prayed for the girl, Jesus told me, "My son, this is your miracle!" Now I had the witness of the Holy Scriptures that the vision was rooted in the Bible, and I had this personal miracle as a sign of my Lord that I was on the right road.

The following Monday night I shared the vision at a prayer meeting of about 180 people in Braunschweig. At first I could not tell if they had received it. They were looking at me as if to say, "Could all this really be possible?" And I didn't know

how to deal with the situation or to interpret their
lack of reaction so I just closed my eyes. I wanted to
feel like an ostrich. I wanted to stick my head in the
sand so everything would disappear. There was no
way to get out of the room. I was standing there with
my eyes closed when that still inner voice of the Lord
said to me, "I want you to go down on your knees and
get on your face before Me."

And I thought, "Oh boy, here I am with 180 Germans looking at me and I'm to get down on my face
before God?" But I had learned how important it is to
obey God, no matter what the circumstances. "Okay,
God," I said. "I'll obey You!" And I got down on my
knees.

Then I heard a noise like that of many people
moving and chairs rustling. I didn't know if they were
coming to get me or if they were running out the door
or what. I opened my eyes a little bit to see what was
going on. And then I realized that every single person
in the room had received the same message from the
Lord. No audible word was spoken, but every single
person was down on their knees and on their faces
before the Lord. Everyone, without exception.

There was an awesome silence. We stayed there
for over twenty minutes. It was a sealing work of the
Holy Spirit. He sealed the vision within our hearts.
Everyone was aware of the deep, deep work of the
Spirit of God within our lives.

We all got up. We didn't speak to each other. We
just filed out and everyone went home. We all knew
God had been there. God's power had been
manifested and the deep work of the Holy Spirit was

accomplished without any words being said. God does not need visible displays or words in order for His glory to accomplish His work within our lives.

Interestingly, the Lord put it on my heart not to talk on a large scale about the vision of the exodus of the Russian Jews. That evening in Braunschweig was the only time I shared the vision publicly for a period of six years. Events had to come into maturity in the redemptive plan of God and in my life before the message could be shared in public.

I now knew that God wanted to lead His people out of Russia, and I sensed the tremendous responsibility the Lord had given me with this knowledge. Therefore, in 1974, a new ministry began in that part of the world. During the next years, I visited all East European countries with the exception of Albania and Bulgaria. During that time, I have been in Russia four times. On one trip I traveled for 17,500 miles back and forth throughout the Soviet Union and as far as Siberia.

This was just in preparation, to get to know the mentality of the people and to find out the different routes to travel. The first two and one half years I worked primarily among persecuted Christians behind the Iron Curtain, holding pastors' conferences, leading youth camps, teaching, and ministering. But at the same time, I tried to find out the situation of the Jews in the Eastern block countries and make contacts.

For the next six years, I was the European Director of the Full Gospel Business Men's Fellowship. I knew almost every major city in both eastern and western Europe like the back of my hand. I wondered why God was having me travel so extensively. But the vision always remained in my heart. I hardly talked about it. I just did not have the green light from the Lord to share it, except on a limited basis.

In October of 1980 I flew to Finland for a series of meetings. It was six years after I had the vision in Braunschweig. Within eleven days, I spoke twenty-nine times. At the end I felt squeezed out like a lemon. On the last day of this trip, I sat in Rauno Kokkola's office, a friend of mine in the central part of Finland, completely exhausted. If it had been possible, I would have flown home immediately. I just did not want to speak anymore. What was I supposed to say after all these days. I groaned, "Jesus, I am at the end of myself, give me words for tonight."

Next to me on the wall was a big map of Finland. Suddenly I saw a fire break out exactly on the border of Russia and Finland. A real fire with flames and smoke. I was wide awake. I looked around me. Where could I get water to quench the fire? But the map did not burn up. Fascinated, I watched the action. "Jesus, what is happening?" I asked.

Again, that quiet well-known voice spoke into my heart, "Do you remember the vision of 1974?" How could I have forgotten all that!

Then I saw the same vision in front of my eyes again. But this time my attention was drawn to more details. I realized, in particular, that the Jews of the northwestern part of Russia did not move toward the super highway via Poland to Western Europe. "Lord, why don't they get on that highway?"

His answer was, "These Jews will come to freedom through Finland. In My grace I will give them the chance to be a blessing to my beloved people."

"Jesus, what shall I do with this new vision?" I asked, deeply moved.

"Haven't you asked Me for a word for tonight's meeting? Here it is. Go and tell this message to the Finnish people!"

Well, I worked up the courage. On this last evening in Finland, I gave the message concerning the exodus of the Jews out of Russia and spoke to them about the responsibility Finland would have.

After the meeting there was a cold silence over the crowd. I was under the impression that they had rejected this message. I wished I could have slipped out a back door and jumped into the next departing airplane. But the reason for the silence was that the message had so impacted them that they just did not know how to react.

Can you imagine the situation I was in? There I stood and wondered what the people were thinking. Had they received the message? Then, five people walked out of the crowd and came to my interpreter. First, an elderly lady. She let me know through the interpreter, "More than forty years ago the Lord spoke to me and said that He will lead the Jews out of Russia via Finland. But He ordered me not to tell anyone about it, until a foreigner comes to our country and publicly speaks about it. Then, Jesus said to me, 'Go immediately to him and confirm it for he will need that!' " And how I needed that!

My interpreter became more excited when the man who stood behind that lady began to tell him that just half a year before he had the impression to buy five storage houses in his city. The Lord had told him that he would host a large number of people. "Presently some of these houses are being used to exhibit cars," he explained, "and another is being used for tennis courts. But all of them have bathrooms and kitchens. All I have to do is put beds inside. Tonight I know that Jesus really talked to me and that these houses are supposed to be for His people on their journey through," he closed.

My heart leapt with gladness. "Thank you, Jesus!" I rejoiced.

The next person described how he was living close to the border of Russia and that some months before the Lord had told him to buy buses and to start a company, for he will have to transport people who need to get through the country. Now he knew that it had not been his imagination, but that God had really talked to him.

The man behind him reported, "God has called me into the ministry of Joseph. Every year I am to store up ten percent of my harvest, for someday there will be people traveling through my country that are in need of food. I have been obedient to the Lord and have already brought in my fourth harvest."

The last person coming up was again an elderly lady who loved the Jews with all her heart. She said, "You know, the Lord ordered me to learn the Russian language. Why should I learn Russian while I would much rather learn Hebrew in order to converse with

God's people?"

"Only a few Jews in Russia know Hebrew, but all of them speak Russian," was my answer.

"Ohhhhhh...," she rejoiced, "then I have a ministry when the Jews come out of Russia! Now I know why I have to learn Russian. Would you agree with me in prayer that God would speak to the hearts of other people to also learn the Russian language?" We stopped and prayed right then.

These five independent testimonies given after this meeting on my last day in Finland were wonderful confirmations concerning the things the Lord had revealed to me. Once again I had the assurance that I was on the right track. I would need that for the future.

CHAPTER 7

BACK TO RUSSIA

After this experience in Finland, through which the Lord impressed me with the reality of the coming Jewish exodus out of Russia, I knew that as the next step I had to go back to Russia. So in the following year of 1981, I made two trips to Russia. I went to prepare the Jews for the upcoming event of these last days.

The reason for one of these trips was a vision. In it I saw myself by a certain fountain in a Russian city as a man walked up to me. His outer appearance looked Jewish. He began talking to me and while conversing with each other we walked away from that place.

This vision along with all the other experiences beforehand encouraged me and my friends, Phil Israelson, John Dunnington, and Tom Miklautsch to travel to Russia. We had addresses of contacts to make. With expectancy we looked in every city that we passed through for a square with a fountain similar to the one I had seen in the vision, but without success. But one day while we were on an organized tour of a certain city, we passed by a square with a fountain exactly like the one I had seen in the vision. My heart began to beat faster and I knew that I had found the right place. When we found an opportunity, we separated ourselves from the sightseeing group and walked back to the square. I asked myself, "What is going to happen now?"

We strolled leisurely across the square and stood next to the fountain. And, sure enough, a man came walking up and started to talk to us. "You surely are from America?"

"Where did you get that idea?" I returned the question.

"Oh," he said, "because you walk free."

I did not really understand what he meant by that, but we continued the conversation. We found out that he was a Jewish engineer. After a few minutes he asked us to leave the square and to take a walk through the streets. I had noticed that he was turning around every so often. "Why are you turning around all the time?" I asked.

"I have to be sure that no one is following us," he replied.

Then I understood the reason why he recognized us as Westerners at the square; it was the way we walked-free. "That's the reason I noticed you," he explained. "I watched you as you were crossing the square. You did not even turn around once. That's how I knew that you were from the West. I was curious and wanted to get to know you."

We walked for about three and a half hours through the streets giving him our testimony. I told him how Jesus became my personal Messiah, that He had changed my life, and that He wanted to do the same for him as well. We also gave him the message that God loves his own people and wants to gather them from every area of the world and return them to their own country.

Never again have I heard from this man. But I am sure that since God brought us together, He will also complete the work in this man's life.

We had the address of a Jewish family living in another city. Their son lives in the U.S.A. and he had asked us to go and visit with them. When we arrived, they called their friends and relatives. We sat down for dinner and they were so happy because we knew their son and we had brought a gift and had reported how he was doing. Then they began to question me, "Tell us, is there another reason for you to be in the Soviet Union?"

So I shared with them concerning my personal Messiah and how God is starting to prepare the nations of the West to assist in bringing about the release of the Jews out of the Soviet Union. I shared with them the Scripture verses and how God had heard the cry of their hearts. I also told them that they should prepare themselves, for it would be a sudden move to freedom and into their promised land. I had not anticipated their reactions. The cry of their heart went in an entirely different direction. They reacted with rejection, accusing me of being a fanatic, having come just to cause difficulty and political problems for them. Nervously, the man of the house jumped up, ran to the telephone, and began to dial a number. Another person walked to the closet, gave us our coats, and motioned us in no uncertain terms to leave immediately.

Even though I insisted again and again that it was not my purpose to cause political problems, they laughed at us with scorn. "You must leave immediately. We don't want any difficulty or any political problems."

In the meantime, a taxi had arrived. That had been the reason for the telephone call, to make us leave quickly. Hastily, they led us down the stairs. Unexpectedly, one of the ladies asked us, "Could you please write down the Bible verses you have mentioned? My father still attends the synagogue and I would like to give them to him." While walking down the stairs, I quickly wrote the Bible verses on a piece of paper and gave it to her.

Then they pushed us into the taxi and we went back to the hotel. Surely this visit did not seem to have been very successful. We committed everything into the Lord's hand and prayed for the family. After we had made a few more inquiries and visits, we left the Soviet Union.

On returning home, I began to make further preparations for a more extended journey through the Soviet Union in order to reach many Jews in various places as the Holy Spirit would lead us. Before the departure, the Lord gave me two directives. One was that I should travel on the Trans

Siberian Railroad. The other was that when I got to
Yalta, I should go down and lie on the beach.

Well, this was a clear instruction from the Lord
and I thought, "That really sounds strange."
However, over the years, I had learned to clearly
distinguish between my own imagination and the
voice of God. So I took these instructions seriously.
During the preparation for the visa and tickets, I told
these impressions to Matt McLallin who would be
traveling with me. "That sounds good to my flesh,"
he replied laughingly.

Our first stop was the same family I had visited a
month earlier. With some anxiety, we went to their
home by taxi. After all, their last farewell was still in
my memory. Surprisingly, they gave us a warm
reception and were very nice all the time we were
with them. We were almost under the impression that
they wanted to make restitution. We found out later
on that the lady to whom I had given the slip of paper
with the Bible verses concerning the exodus of the
Jews, had indeed given it to her father. Together with
the other men in the synagogue, he had looked the Bible verses up and had written them down in Russian,
Hebrew, and Yiddish. As a little gift, they handed us
the slips of paper with the Bible verses written in the
three languages. My first reaction was, "What shall I
do with them? I can't read them." But the Spirit of
the Lord said, "Take them, you will need them."

In another city we stayed three days, looking up
addresses and making contacts. We rose early one
morning and needed hours just to get into a particular
region of the town. After a long search, we found the

specific house and rang the doorbell, but nobody came to the door. Waiting awhile we thought, "Too bad, they must be on vacation or perhaps they are out shopping."

Since we were not successful, we decided to return to our hotel. On our way back, we looked up another address and found the place in the back of another building. We had to go through a very dark gateway and then climb up six flights of stairs. As we knocked on the door, a lady one floor below opened her door. We waited, hoping she would go downstairs. We did not want to be recognized as foreigners. But no, she started walking upstairs at exactly the same moment that the owner of the apartment opened his door. He immediately recognized the situation, spoke in Russian, and joyfully stretched out his arm and with a friendly gesture pulled us into his home. It was good that we had not spoken to him in English at the door and revealed our identity as foreigners.

When we talked to him about the other address, he said, "It's good that you did not reach anybody. Three months ago the Jews living at that place had received their permission to leave the country. Now somebody else lives there. If they had been at home they surely would have notified the police." We were glad that we had been protected and able to make this new contact. It did not take us long to get acquainted. So he decided to take us along with him to his synagogue. The building was small and at the edge of the city. According to Jewish law, a worship service is only permitted if ten Jewish men are present.

The leader counted and together with the both of us, we were ten.

Once again we were able to pass on our message and had receptive listeners. They already knew the Bible passages and asked time and again, "When will it happen?" All I could tell them was that I did not know and could not give them any time, but that God has been speaking to many different people in the West to make preparations and be ready to help them.

They were comforted to hear that the purpose of our travel was to let them know, so they also could prepare. Since one of the men present was a key person with contacts in other synagogues, this had really been a moment of God's leading.

Traveling through a few other cities, we finally came to Yalta. Since the last few days really had put a strain on us, we were pleased with the idea that God had told us to go and lie on the beach.

I could not believe my eyes the next morning as I looked out of the hotel window. Multitudes of people were streaming towards the beach; it was an unbelievable scene. I thought that all Russia must have come to the beach. Nowhere else in all the world had I seen that many people on a beach, not even in Hawaii or Florida. Later on I read in a brochure that annually 8,500,000 Russians would spend their vacation in this area of Russia.

So we began walking along the beach promenade to find a place to lie down. Finally we found one just large enough for two people. When we put down our bathing towels, our feet almost touched the heads of

the men before us and our heads were at the feet of
two ladies, who were sitting with their backs against
the beach wall.

Here we were in the only empty space we found.
"Lord, You have said we should lie on the beach. Here
we are! What comes next?" I really could not explain
what the whole thing was about. But it was nice to lie
in the sun. The last days had almost exhausted us and
now I just about dozed off. Half asleep, I heard the
two ladies behind us speaking in Russian. Although I
don't even know the Russian language, it sounded as
if they were mentioning the words "Israel" and
"synagogue." Suddenly, I was wide awake. Could it
be that they were Jews? Matt had heard the same
thing and leaned over to catch more of what the ladies
were saying.

They had noticed our interest and asked us in
Russian if we could understand them. Matt managed
to explain that he could understand them but that his
ability to speak Russian was very limited. Now they
knew that we were foreigners. They seemed to be a
bit fearful, and yet curious at the same time. We
showed them postcards from our hometowns and
tried to make clear our purpose for being there. To no
avail. Suddenly, it came into my mind....the slips of
paper! "Matt," I said, "quick! Run to the hotel and
get those Bible verses we have in three languages."

"I don't have to," he said. "I've got them right
here." I have hardly ever seen anybody so excited as
when we handed the women those verses. They
wanted to read the papers immediately but did not
dare, because of all the people behind them walking

along the beach. When they realized that there were Bible passages on those slips, they looked around even more fearfully.

Finally, they took their towels on which they had been sitting, pulled them over their heads, and began reading these Bible verses in the secrecy of this covering. Again and again they expressed in Russian, "Bible." It was obvious that they understood this Bible text. They beamed all over and made clear to us that they would like to take the papers with them to their synagogues. We also found that those synagogues were in an area of Russia where we were not permitted to travel.

After this experience we could really relax with the confidence that the Lord had surely led us to this beach. How thankful we were that we had obeyed the Lord to go and lie on the beach, without the slightest idea of His purpose.

It is amazing how God arranges circumstances! What a miracle that on an over-populated beach like this we met key people like those two Jewish women. How important it is to know the voice of God so that His plans and purposes can be fulfilled.

Well rested, we could continue on our journey. But regardless of the highlights of our trip, there were situations which were uneventful and did not seem to produce any results. We traveled through some cities without any successful contacts at all.

Then we got on the Trans Siberian Railroad as the Lord had told us to do. It was an exciting trip. For eight and a half days we were on the train. During the first four days we were wondering what might come our way.

Then it came. In Irkutsk, Siberia, many people boarded the train. Matt was standing at the open door of our small compartment as other travelers were passing by. Suddenly a very strongly built man stood in front of my friend and screamed with a loud voice, "Boris! Boris!" He grabbed Matt by the shoulders, shook him, and spoke rapidly to him in Russian. Startled by the noise, I stepped out and said to myself, "If that is not a Jew....!" Immediately, he began to talk exuberantly with me. I raised my hands to motion that I could not understand one word. Then he asked whether I knew German. I replied in Yiddish, "A little." That was the only word I knew in the Yiddish language. I did this to see if he was really a Jew. With a broad smile and great excitement, Yiddish words flooded out of his mouth. But I don't know how to speak Yiddish at all. So we talked with one another by motioning with hands and arms.

Soon he seated himself in our compartment with a smile on his face. In the meantime, we had found out that he was a Jew and he knew that I was a Jew. And then a miracle happened. The anointing of the Holy Spirit came over me so that suddenly I was able to understand what he was saying in Yiddish. Matt looked at me with wide eyes as I translated for him the words of our guest.

For seven hours we continued our conversation. Each of us shared out of his life and experience, for I found that I could not only understand Yiddish, but by the power of the Holy Spirit was also able to speak Yiddish. Finally Matt said, "You don't have to translate anymore, unless I have a special question, because I too am able to understand him."

Our new friend, Janish, began telling us about his relatives. As a whole family they had applied for permission to leave the country for Israel. Finally his parents and his sister were allowed to leave under great hardship, but he had to stay, thereby becoming a refusnik, one who has been denied permission to leave the Soviet Union.

The reason he had called my partner "Boris" was that he looked so similar to his best friend who had been permitted to leave Russia three years before. Janish had thought he had returned for a visit, and could not believe it. So again, God had brought us in contact in a special way with this man.

We shared with him out of our experiences, our faith in our personal Messiah, and our calling to Russia. He was so delighted to hear that God had heard the cry of His people and is preparing the way for them to return to their land. Time and again he jumped up and, because the compartment was too small, he opened the door and paced back and forth in the corridor. He would return, close the door and say, "Tell me more! Tell me more!" All our words fell on a prepared heart.

For the remaining four days of this train ride, we spent a lot of time together. The train was overcrowded. Therefore, the other passengers became aware of our friendship with Janish. He had to stay with nine people in a four bed compartment and therefore slept on the floor.

Next to our compartment was a family which had

to change quarters very suddenly one night. A young lady moved in all by herself, and immediately the next morning she tried to make contact with us. She spoke English quite well and seemed to be very interested in my younger friend Matt. Constantly she asked questions. Since he had suspicions about her interest in him, he was smart enough to get out his camera and take pictures all along the way. He explained to her that we were traveling as tourists and were putting together a series of slides. When he asked her if she had had a vacation, it slipped out of her, "Oh yes, last year in Cuba." Right then she bit her tongue. Only members of the Communist party are allowed to go to Cuba.

The other Russians on the train had warned Janish that this woman had been asking many questions about us and now we knew that we must be very careful in our conversation. That lady tried every trick she could think of. Again and again she invited Matt into her compartment and made several enticing offers. But our Lord knew how to stop her.

The train stopped in the open country for several hours because of some construction on the tracks. One of the passengers ran into the woods and returned with a little pail of berries. After a while the young lady asked Matt again to come to her compartment for some berries. But he made excuses. In the evening we sat together with Janish and asked him about the woman since we had not seen her for a while. He smiled, "The berries she ate were not edible. Now she is sick in bed and can't get up." Surely enough, we did not see her again till the end of the trip.

We endeavored to help Janish to get out of the overloaded compartment. In our car was one free bed, but the price was so staggeringly high that we could not even pay for it for him. But then Janish saw a five-blade pack of Gilette razor blades in one of our cases. This was nothing special for us nor of much value. His eyes grew wide and he said, "If I could have those, I can get the bed." Sure enough, those five razor blades were of more value to the stewardess of our car than a great sum of money. Janish got the bed in our car.

Each of us had brought along a suit on the trip. Matt felt impressed by the Lord to give his to Janish. It fit him perfectly, as if it had been tailor-made. "I have never had a suit that really fit me!" he exclaimed. He recognized that God had indeed sent us, that God knew his personal situation and even the size of his suit. He decided to remain with us as we continued on to various cities. He came with us on the buses and into hotels which are off limits to Russians. When he wanted to carry my suitcase, I objected at first. But then I understood. With that luggage and suit, he really looked like someone from the West. No one would suspect that he was Russian. So, we really had a good time together, looking like tourists.

Again and again he wanted to hear our report concerning the exodus of the Jews out of Russia. Then he begged us to write everything down, the vision, the confirmations from other people, the preparations in other nations, and, most of all, the Bible passages.

When we began to write, we found that we almost had a small book. Janish had obviously been prepared by God and it was his desire to share these experiences with others. He wanted to have everything on paper because he was worried that he might forget some of it. And a Jewish friend of his was able to translate it from English into Russian.

When Janish had applied for permission to go to Israel, he had been rejected and even lost his job and was demoted. Now he had to travel as a purchasing agent for his factory to various cities to look for the materials they needed for production. Almost every day he was on the road.

We realized that even though Satan had tried to hamper him, God had turned it into good. Because of his position, he was able to travel everywhere and could tell this message to the Jews in many cities, especially in those many areas where we could never go. This man became one of the most important contacts for us in Russia, especially for the territories east of Moscow.

Later, we had the opportunity of visiting Janish's parents in Israel. What a joy it was to bring personal greetings from him and show them pictures of Janish. They also showed us a picture of Boris, Janish's best friend. Surely, he looked very similar to Matt. It was not surprising that Janish had mistaken Matt for Boris. God used this mistaken identity so that we could have the opportunity to get the message out to many people in Russia through Janish.

During this journey, we covered 17,500 miles and reached Jews in many cities of the Soviet Union. We

met key people on the streets, in the synagogues, on
the beach, in homes, and on the train; they continue to
carry the message on. This trip had truly been
motivated and guided by the Holy Spirit. In the meantime I have met other people from the West who have
traveled the Soviet Union with basically the same
message.They continually contact many other people
so that we can estimate that quite a percentage of the
Jewish people have been informed about God's plan.

CHAPTER 8
PASS IT ON!

After all these travels in Russia, God showed me that we should establish our home in Israel. In the beginning of 1982, we moved there and now live in Jerusalem.

In the past, God had only allowed me to speak publicly four times in the West on the prophetic word concerning the Jews in Russia. The first time was in August, 1974, in a prayer group in Braunschweig just after I had the vision of the highway. The second time was in Finland in 1980 after I had seen in a vision the burning border between Russia and Finland. The other two were in September, 1981, at the FGBMFI German National Convention in Dusseldorf and at the Feast of Succoth (Tabernacles) in 1982 in Jerusalem where I was a guest speaker.

However, at the end of 1982 the Holy Spirit witnessed to me, "The time of restricted sharing is passed. Proclaim it in all the world so that all may know and prepare!"

I made a trip around the world at the beginning of 1983 to bring this message to the nations. Starting in Holland, Germany, Belgium, Denmark, Sweden, and Finland, the trip continued via Australia, the United States and Canada and back to Israel. I have been surprised that in almost every city, wherever I have spoken, people have come up and testified that the Lord had already given them this message and they just wanted to confirm that I was on the right track with this ministry.

I have met with spiritual leaders in several countries and heard with amazement that they also had received from the Lord, independently of me, the same message: that the Jews will come out of Russia. These are tremendous confirmations.

The greatest surprise I had was in Finland. We had meetings in twenty-three cities and I spoke to thousands of people. During this time more than 200 people received Jesus and over 1400 Christians received the baptism in the Holy Spirit.

About 40% of prophecy in the Old Testament was directed at cities and nations. For instance, Jonah was called of God to speak to and warn the city of Ninevah. Other prophets were called to speak to the whole nation of Israel or even to other nations, not just individuals. Therefore, I was excited when I received an invitation to speak to representatives of Parliament at the Finnish Parliament building. It was an opportunity to call that nation to its prophetic role in the last days. I didn't pull any punches. There was a press conference and the message made the headlines on the front pages of the Finnish newspapers. Even BBC broadcast the same report twice one day later over their worldwide network. This means it reached the people who needed to hear it the most, those in Europe and Israel.

The preparations in Finland are more advanced than in any other country. I have actually seen many places where preparations have been made. While in Finland, I daily met people who had already heard this same message from God before they had ever met or heard of me.

How good it is of the Lord to keep on confirming the vision that He has given me. I am excited as I travel and hear about the preparations that the Lord has initiated all along the routes of the coming exodus. But I believe God wants everyone to know about His plans to bring His people out of Russia and from around the world, to take them back to the Promised Land. I see my ministry as a voice crying in the wilderness: "Prepare Ye the Way of the Lord!" I am encouraging everyone I talk with to share the vision with others--to pass it on!

PART II

PROPHETIC PREPARATION IN EUROPE

Compiled by Eberhard Muehlan

CHAPTER 9

SEARCHING OUT THE TRUTH

Compiled by Eberhard Muehlan

What can come out of a book when a skeptic is being requested to write it? Not that I had any doubt concerning the experiences and statements of Steve Lightle — after all, I had known him for over ten years and been with him on some of his outreach journeys. But the visions he was talking about now, concerning the things God had revealed to individual people independently in various countries like Holland, Denmark, Sweden, and Finland, about the exodus of the Jews out of the Soviet Union, sounded so incredible to me that it was hard to believe.

Many people have been hurt in prophetic matters. I did not want to get too involved. It seemed to be more secure to be a spectator and just watch from a distance and see whether it would come to pass or not. But God had other ideas.

When Steve mentioned to me that God had told him to write a book on the subject, I shared some of

my experience with him. I had written a few books
and gave him some advice on how to structure the
book, thinking that would be good enough. Then the
Lord began to work on my heart, "It is not enough to
give Steve advice. Sit down and write the book for
him!"

I did not like this suggestion at all. "Lord, you
know my busy schedule and plans. And after all, I
don't want to have my name associated with such a
controversial subject! What if all this turns out to be
imagination? What if Steve is mistaken and the whole
thing pops like a balloon that has been punctured by a
needle? Then I will be the one who is going to look
really ridiculous!"

I tried to brush the whole idea aside, but I could
not. The task burned like fire within me. And then
during our family devotions, we read these verses out
of Jeremiah 20:7-9, *"O Lord, Thou has deceived me
and I was deceived; Thou hast overcome me and
prevailed. I have become a laughingstock all day long;
everyone mocks me. For each time I speak, I cry aloud;
I proclaim violence and destruction, because for me
the word of the Lord has resulted in reproach and
derision all day long. But if I say, 'I will not
remember Him or speak anymore in His name,' then
in my heart it becomes like a burning fire shut up in
my bones; and I am weary of holding it in, and I cannot endure it."*

I could really imagine the situation in which
Jeremiah had been. He knew the difficulty of his calling and what it would bring into his life. But Jeremiah
was overcome by the love of God and his burning

desire to be obedient to Him. It burned like fire within him so that he was obedient in following God's call.

Suddenly I recognized that my challenge was very similar to that of Jeremiah and these verses became God's "rhema" — a personal word of God for me. That was my situation. I had my own plans and ideas of what I was going to do during the first half of 1983. Then came the request to write this book. I realized that my worry was ridiculous. Despite all my doubts, I had only one desire in my heart — to do the things that are born out of the heart of God. The call still burned like a fire in me that I could not extinguish and the love of the Lord convinced me to be obedient.

Still, I was not satisfied. How should I get hold of such a prophetic subject? How can prophecy be judged realistically, to discern what is from man and what is of God? The reader will surely share with me the anxiety of this question. Many times I had heard prophecies that were never fulfilled. I also thought of some of the spooky sermons individual "prophets" had preached time and again in recent years that the Russians would conquer West Germany. They even gave dates but nothing ever came to pass. The only thing that happened was that unstable Christians became scared and therefore hindered in their actions instead of following Jesus with liberty. Some even took preparatory measures expecting the worst, but it turned out that they were operating in the flesh and not from God's orders. Surely, God does not speak in order to bring confusion.

One night, while I was restless and these

thoughts were going through my mind, the Lord gave me a key verse for the discernment of prophecy. It also worked out to be the structure of this book. "Look, my son," the Lord said to me, "there are at least three witnesses concerning the exodus of the Jews out of the Soviet Union. In Jeremiah and other prophetic books, My Word testifies about the release of My people out of the country of the north. Then there is your brother Steve Lightle, to whom I have spoken already in 1974, and the third group of witnesses are the many people in various nations to whom I have independently revealed the same things."

I was really relieved as these thoughts were brought clearly to my mind. If the Bible did not unmistakably testify about the coming out of God's people from "the land of the north," I would have to take my hands off the project immediately. But when I examined the Scriptures, it was all there. Jeremiah 23:7,8 says, " *'Therefore behold, the days are coming,' declares the Lord, 'when they will no longer say, "As the Lord lives, who brought up the sons of Israel from the land of Egypt," but "As the Lord lives who brought up and led back the descendants of the household of Israel from the north land and from all the countries where I had driven them." Then they will live on their own soil.' "*

The same Holy Spirit who inspired the Bible also speaks to man. He will never contradict Himself by saying something which does not agree with what has been already revealed in the Bible. If we hear any kind of prophecy, it will have to be in agreement with biblical thought patterns and must be verified in the Bible.

Surely all Bible-believing Christians will agree that the Bible indeed testifies to the coming exodus of the Jews out of "the country of the north." The only point of discussion can be: when will it happen? Isn't it remarkable to hear that God has not been talking to just one person but has been revealing the same thing to many Christians in various countries? If we had only one person, for instance Steve Lightle, who proclaimed the matter, it would not be dependable enough. But if there are many others to whom God has spoken in a personal way, then the whole picture will be more dependable and stands on more solid ground.

I was interested in these people and made plans for a trip to study the situation, to make interviews, and to really check out where their knowledge originated. "I will dare to write the book," I said to myself, "if I shall find dependable testimonies which will be real confirmations to a genuine, prophetic utterance of God."

In February and March of 1983, I began to travel to the countries of Denmark, Sweden, Finland, Holland, and Germany, visiting with the Christians who had claimed to have heard from God about the exodus of the Jews out of the Soviet Union. I found that everything was beyond my expectations in relation to the prophetic revelations. This made out of a skeptic a person now convinced of the truth of these reports.

We are living in a decisive period of history in

God's redemptive plan in which Jesus is preparing His church around the world for the fulfillment of another important end-time prophecy. Some of the end-time prophecies have already come to pass, like the founding of the state of Israel in May of 1948 (Isaiah 66:8) and the liberation of the old city of Jerusalem in June of 1967 (Luke 21:24), so we can expect the release of His people out of the "country of the north" and the worldwide homecoming of the Jews into their land.

Even though some of the localities and names have had to be changed for the protection of people I interviewed, I have used the actual, verifiable reports of these eyewitnesses. In this book I have only included reports that either Steve Lightle or I or reliable eyewitnesses who are personally known to us have proven to be true. We have many reports from other people that we have chosen not to publish because we were not able to check them out to verify them. It is our sincere desire to present only proven facts so that the reader can depend on our report.

CHAPTER 10

FINLAND

Compiled by Eberhard Muehlan

The preparation of the Holy Spirit for Finland in relation to all the other countries impressed me the most. For several days I had the opportunity to be part of the meetings there with Steve Lightle and to interview many Christians. There were tremendous turnouts at the meetings. People came by bus loads from far distant places in Finland. Over the years God has spoken to literally hundreds of Christians about being prepared for the great exodus of the Russian Jews. For them the message Steve presented was nothing new, but a personal confirmation for what God already had told them.

In one meeting in a particular city I had four people come to me afterwards, confirming to me the message Steve Lightle had just given. God had told one farmer thirteen years ago that many of the Jews coming out of Russia would travel through Finland on their way to Israel. Five years ago the Holy Spirit had spoken to him about this for the second time. Then he became serious about it and purchased a farm in order to be able to help in a practical way when the time arose.

Two other persons with beaming faces told me through the interpreter that they had had the same vision as Steve's some years ago and now they were glad that a foreigner had come to confirm it.

The fourth person to come to me after the meeting was a lady who had begun to learn Russian a few years ago. She had been under the impression it would enable her to be of help to Jews coming out of the Soviet Union.

So one report after the other lined up in confirmation. I was impressed with the great number of Christians who have been learning Russian for some time now. We found a group of over sixty people who come together regularly just to learn the Russian language. In every one of the twenty-three cities where Steve spoke at least one, and many times up to five people, testified that God had put it on their heart to learn the Russian language.

One lady came up to us after a meeting, all excited, telling us, "I am a teacher and last fall (1982) I started to learn Russian without being sure why. Professionally I don't need that language. Two colleagues of mine who are also Christians started learning Russian two years ago. They also sensed that God wanted them to do it. Tonight it really became clear to me why I must learn this language. I am so glad that some day I will be able to talk with Jews from Russia and in their own language. I will be able to say 'Here is my house,' or 'Welcome,' and I will tell them about my Savior Jesus."

During my stay in Finland, I also met the interpreter who had translated for Steve at that special meeting in October 1980 when five people came forward to give their confirmations to him. The interpreter again confirmed the validity of all those testimonies. He also mentioned that the person to whom God had spoken concerning the buses to transport the people through the country had died. His son had taken over and purchased even more buses. He now runs a Christian travel business with one thought in mind, to maintain those vehicles for the eventual transportation of the Russian Jews through Finland.

I visited in person the man who had mentioned to Steve that God had told him to buy five warehouses. He confirmed that God had spoken to him before he got to know Steve at that meeting in October of 1980. "You know," he said, "I've always had love for the Jewish people. When I had the opportunity to buy these five warehouses, I was under the impression that some day I would host a multitude of people. When I heard the message of Steve Lightle, I was sure that only the Jews from out of the Soviet Union could have been meant by this impression."

I found out that because of business difficulties, it had been necessary to sell some of those buildings. He kept one of them that is now an automobile showroom with a restaurant, many showers, sauna, toilets, and car repair shop adjacent to it. "On top of that, I own two buses, a large seaworthy boat, a summer house,

and my own house which shall all be used for the
Lord's purpose," he exclaimed.

We spent an extended amount of time interview-
ing a Jewish couple, completed Jews, living on a farm
near the Russian border. We had heard that they
were preparing to receive the Soviet Jews. Steve had
visited them before and had looked over everything.
Now I had the opportunity to visit them myself and to
interview the husband.

Eberhard: When did you move to this farm and what
  was the reason for it?

Pekka: In the fall of 1977 we sold our business in
  Helsinki and purchased this old farm with all
  these buildings. We took this step because God
  had told us to prepare a place of rest for difficult
  times and where people can find refuge.

Eberhard: So, at that time you did not have the impression that this project would be for Russian
  Jews?

Pekka: No, this idea came later. We had thought
  about alcoholics or drug addicts. We had just
  begun to renovate this old place. On a Sabbath in
  September of 1980, we were sitting in the kitchen and praying. As my wife looked up out on
  the lawn in front of our house the Lord began to
  speak to her heart, "For many people this place
  will some day be like Calvary." And then she had
  a vision: Many poorly dressed people came in
  crowds out of the direction of the Russian border
  through the woods and across the meadow in
  front of our house looking for refuge. This is all

she saw, but it really impressed us.

Eberhard: But this vision did not show that these were Jews coming out of the Soviet Union?

Pekka: That is right. We did not interpret it that way. To be honest, we really did not know what to do with that vision. Later, a friend of my wife gave us a cassette with the message of Steve Lightle about the exodus of the Jews out of the Soviet Union. That's when we began to comprehend my wife's vision and the Holy Spirit told us, "Now you know who these people are for whom you shall prepare a refuge and minister unto them!"

Eberhard: If I understood you correctly, you had never before heard from Steve Lightle or any other person concerning the exodus of the Jews?

Pekka: Yes, my wife's vision occurred in September of 1980. Steve Lightle spoke in Finland one month later. We did not attend that meeting, but received the cassette tape of it later.

Eberhard: Did you take any further action of preparation after that?

Pekka: We did some reconstruction on our house and now have space for fifty to sixty people. Then there is space for about fifteen more people in the shed. In addition, we have a large barn and a storage building for emergency quarters. We are storing a lot of clothes and shoes. The farm produces some wheat, potatoes, and vegetables. At the present time, we are using the facilities for the rehabilitation of drug and alcohol addicts, but we are ready at any time to adapt everything for its original purpose.

Eberhard: Have you ever harbored any doubt about this project?

Pekka: Surely! That is to be expected. Since we had many difficulties during the reconstruction period, doubts arose and we prayed, "Lord, send us a confirmation!" Once a sister in the Lord gave us a confirmation through a prophecy. Then in June of 1982, as we were feeling rather depressed, a group of young Christians came to our house and through the Holy Spirit confirmed that the vision was of the Lord. We received courage to continue the work.

Eberhard: Do you know other people who have received the same calling from God?

Pekka: Oh yes, there are many. Especially here in the border region God has spoken to quite a few. I know about one woman who owns a resort and she is convinced that someday she will take in Jewish refugees. Also, a good friend of ours, who lives about twenty miles away, developed a farm for animals two years ago and he has the same calling to help the Russian Jews someday.

This neighbor, mentioned above by the man, was glad when Steve visited him. He had heard Steve for the first time at the meeting in October 1980 and told him, "You know, it is pretty difficult when you are under the impression that you are the only one who has received a message. Some months before I heard your message, God had told me to start raising animals in order to have food for the Jews from Russia. Many people advised me against it and thought that I was crazy. Their cautions did not stop me.

"Then I came to the meeting and heard you tell how God is preparing for a great exodus of His Jewish people out of Russia. Since that evening I have no longer been the same. Now I know that it was not my imagination and that God does not lie. Later on, I got to know my neighbor that you've just interviewed and we confirmed to each other our common calling."

We met many other farmers who in very practical ways are preparing and storing up food.

A dairy and beef farmer told us that a few years ago he had wondered whether or not he should stay in the farming business and so he prayed, "Lord, why must I be a farmer? Couldn't I minister unto You much better as an evangelist or in some other way in the kingdom of God?"

But the Lord answered him, "Stay a farmer, for in the future you will be able to help other believers and the Jews." In the spring of 1980, half a year before he heard Steve's message, he saw in a vision Russian Jews traveling through Finland.

Although the spring was very cold and he could not expect a good harvest, he asked the Lord to bless the harvest, and He did. So he was able to store large amounts of wheat in different places. This also enables him to increase the number of his cattle. Smiling, he added, "I am preserving beef on the hoof." He also told us that many farmers in the area are doing the same thing and they are meeting now twice a week with six to eight couples for prayer, especially to intercede for the liberation of the Jews in the Soviet Union.

Another person told Steve that in 1974 God had told him to build a large elevator for grain storage. He began in 1975 and hopes to be finished by August of 1983. Each section will hold about 253 cubic meters (about 500 tons) of grain. He too heard about Steve's vision in October 1980 and was now assured of the purpose for building the grain elevator.

Others told me that they are preparing accommodations. The president of a Bible school said, "When the exodus happens, we will shut down the school immediately and will have space for one hundred people."

Various churches declared that they are prepared to make their church camps available, some of which will hold from 500 to 1000 people.

Many Christians testified in very simple terms that their home would be open for the Russian Jews. One elderly man, for instance, told me after a meeting, "Thank you for this message! Two years ago the Lord had put it on my heart to pray for the Jews in Russia. Now this explains the reason for it. Our children are all gone and my wife and I are living alone in our big house. When the time comes for the exodus, we will surely be able to take in two Jewish families." Many people in Finland are thinking like that.

We found some Christians whom the Lord had told to get one or more Russian Bibles. One man reported that four years ago he had worked behind the Iron Curtain and had tried to smuggle 25,000 Russian Bibles into Russia, but he was not able to get all of them in. Presently, he still has 10,000 Russian

Bibles in storage. "We always questioned, why was it not possible to get those Bibles in? Now we know that they were held back for the Russian Jews."

A member of the Finnish parliament who is a Christian gave his testimony at one of the meetings. "Believers had told me of this message about the exodus of the Jews out of the Soviet Union before," he said, "but I doubted it. After what I have heard tonight, and since this message is obviously biblical, my unbelief is gone and I want to help where I can."

This parliamentarian made it possible for Steve to speak for one hour to members of the Finnish parliament, concluding with a press conference. This public appearance made it possible for Steve's message to make the headlines of six of the largest Finnish newspapers, and everybody in Finland has now had the possibility of getting the information about the predicted exodus of the Russian Jews.

Immediately following Steve's speech in the Parliament, a time was given for questions to be asked. Another member of Parliament, who earlier had appeared to be uninterested, stood up and said, "I have just returned from my home city where my phone has hardly stopped ringing as people called to make arrangements to receive the Jews as they come out of Russia.

"For instance," he said, "one couple that I know well, who have no children, showed me a whole garage full of children's clothing that they were saving for Jewish families. I confirm that what Steve Lightle has said is true and we'd better listen to what God is saying to our nation and obey Him."

There were no more questions.

Impressed by Steve's speech, a man came up and said to him, "I would like to tell you this as a confirmation. A friend of mine has a prophetic ministry. Five or six years ago he told me that Finland will be important for the Russian Jews because one day they will come through our country on their way to Israel. He also said that we must pray that the borders will remain open. At that time I thought he was crazy and did not think it could be possible for such an exodus to take place. But he told me, 'Just wait, the time will come, there will be many Jews traveling through Finland and will then move on to Israel.' Today, I have heard your message and I can see that it agrees perfectly with the one my friend received prophetically years ago."

CHAPTER 11

SWEDEN

Compiled by Eberhard Muehlan

The situation in Sweden will be reflected most adequately by the interview I had with Pastor Kjell Sjoberg from Stockholm:

Eberhard: Rev. Sjoberg, when was it that you were confronted for the first time with the subject of the exodus of the Jews out of the Soviet Union?

Kjell: As a pastor, I have always been interested in the subject of Israel. But I first heard about the Jews coming out of the Soviet Union through a prophetic word at a prayer meeting. It was like a sudden inspiration.

Eberhard: When did that happen?

Kjell: In March of 1982. As "Intercessors for Sweden" we had gathered for a day of prayer with about thirty to forty believers at the City Church in Stockholm.

Eberhard: You were together for a whole day of prayer? Who are the "Intercessors for Sweden"?

Kjell: Yes, we meet every last Monday of the month
for a whole day of prayer, interceding especially
for our government and other prayer requests.
The "Intercessors," as we are called, are an international group represented in many countries.
We come together from many different churches
and are in contact with ecumenical prayer
groups.

Eberhard: Please explain to me how you received this
"prophetic word."

Kjell: As I mentioned, we had been in prayer all day
and interceded for the different prayer requests.
Then in the afternoon I had the sudden inspiration to lay all other requests aside and just pray
for the Jews in the Soviet Union. As I expressed
that suggestion, some began immediately to pray
in the Spirit and to prophesy. It was as if a prophetic mantle had fallen over the whole group.
For about one and a half hours, we received prophetic inspiration. Almost everyone had a special
leading in prayer, a word of prophecy, or a vision.

Some of the people praying began to take
authority over the spiritual powers controlling
the Soviet Union, "Give up, give up, you Pharaoh
of Soviet Russia! In the name of Jesus Christ of
Nazareth, we command you, you wild beast of the
Soviet Union, let the people of God go, for the
time has come for God's people to leave the
Soviet Union!"

The Holy Spirit led us in our prayers and
made God's plans for the future clear to our
minds. We prayed for the leader of the Soviet

Union who will be the successor of Breshnev,
that he will bow to the will of God and permit the
Jews to leave the country.

Eberhard: If this prayer meeting took place in March
of 1982, then this prayer must have been for the
present secretary of the Communist Party, Yuri
Andropov?

Kjell: Yes, that is the interesting part of it. At that
time we had no idea that Mr. Breshnev would die
in November of 1982, and that Mr. Andropov
would be put in office as secretary of the Communist Party. This man has fifteen years of experience with the KGB (Soviet secret police) and
therefore can very well be compared with a type
of Pharaoh.

There were more specific details that we
were impressed to include in our prayers. We
prayed that ministries would be raised up like
that of Moses among the Jews and the Christians, with signs similar to those that Moses and
Aaron did in Egypt. We also prayed that the
Jews in the Soviet Union would be prepared for
the move and that it all would happen very quickly. We asked the Lord to miraculously open up
the routes of travel, as He had done for the
Israelites as they crossed the Red Sea. Suddenly,
we felt led to pray that the route through Austria
would be closed and the route from Leningrad via
Finland to Sweden and on by airplanes to Israel
would be opened. Later on we heard that Israel
had considered that the Soviet Jews should no
longer take the travel route through Austria.

This was especially because of the relationships of Chancellor Bruno Kreisky with Yassir Arafat and Qaddafi. We were led to pray for our Swedish politicians. It is important that they are willing to assist the Soviet Jews in permitting them to travel through Sweden. We were praying that the churches and individual Christians would prepare themselves so that they would be able to help the Jews on their way through. While we were in prayer, many received prophetic messages, some had visions, and others a word from the Bible. We experienced how a whole group of people could be moved by the spirit of prophecy.

Eberhard: The statements you have just made all compare exactly with the prophetic word that Steve Lightle had received. Did you know Steve Lightle or had you heard his message before March of 1982?

Kjell: I did not know Steve Lightle nor had I known anything about his vision. As I was speaking on this subject at a meeting in Narvik, Norway, in April of 1982, someone came to me after the meeting and said, "I have heard before what you have just been talking about." He gave me a cassette with the message of Steve Lightle on it. So, one month after our prayer meeting I found out that God had given Steve the same message. Later on in September of 1982 I met Steve Lightle in Jerusalem and we had a personal exchange.

Eberhard: So you are testifying that you received all these leadings through inspiration of God without any information from other people beforehand?

Kjell: Exactly, that's how it was!

Eberhard: After you had received the confirmation from Steve's message in April, what concrete steps did you take?

Kjell: I am convinced that the Christians in Sweden have a special prophetic ministry in connection with the exodus of the Jews out of the Soviet Union. We did not receive this prophecy in order to sit back and wait passively for the fulfillment. No, the Lord gave the prophecy so that we would have guidance on how we can work with Him so that the prophecy will be fulfilled.

Our first step has been to send a letter of prayer requests to all the members of the "Intercessors for Sweden." We have a list of about 7,000 addresses of people who belong to or lead a prayer fellowship. In this letter we shared our vision with them and challenged them to intercede with us for the Jews in the Soviet Union and Israel.

Secondly, I wrote a detailed letter to all the 550 pastors of my denomination with some specific advice on how to pray in their worship services for the Russian Jews and also how to teach and preach about the prophetic word concerning Israel. We will need to watch that the Body of Christ will not be poisoned by the anti-Israel propaganda of the mass media. Our teaching about the specific role of Israel in prophecy will work to neutralize such propaganda. I asked them to follow closely the development in the mass media about the situation of the Jews in the Soviet Union. Also, I suggested that they should write to the members of the Swedish Parliament and the politicians on all levels. Our politicians must know that there is strength in the number of Christians that support the repressed Jews. Finally, I encouraged them to be open for unexpected prophetic happenings of any kind.

As a third concrete step, we had special days of prayer in twenty cities in preparation for our political elections. During those days we prayed especially for the government and the Jews in the Soviet Union. Many Christians were drawn into spiritual battle in prayer at these meetings.

Eberhard: You took quite a few actions in the period of one year! If I understood you correctly, your actions were more of a verbal or spiritual nature, in the form of prayer and information. Are there Christians in your country who are preparing themselves in a practical way to receive the Jews, like the many people I have met in Finland?

Kjell: I am aware of the situation in Finland but I think that the points of impact are different for the believers in Sweden. Certainly I don't know everything about the situation in Sweden, but I do know of some cases where, for instance, housing is being prepared and food stored.

I believe that at the present time in Sweden the spiritual preparation of the Christians and the spiritual warfare is more important. This is how the Holy Spirit directed us and He will speak to us again if He has other things in mind.

Eberhard: If I think about the three steps you have taken like the letter of prayer concern to 7,000 believers, the information to 550 pastors, and the days of prayer in twenty different cities, I can picture that these people also have passed on the message. This means that you have reached a respectable portion of the population. Did the public or the politicians react at all?

Kjell: Oh yes! The prayers for our government and our politicians were one of the main points on our prayer list and we had real answers to these prayers. We do have some parliamentarians who have a real heart for the Russian Jews. Several parties had sent representatives into the Soviet Union and they reported back later on. During the meeting of the Parliament on April 20, 1982 the parliamentarian, Bonnie Bernstrom, asked some questions to the foreign minister, Ola Ulsten, which opened the debate. She asked, "How does the government evaluate the present situation of the Jews in the Soviet Union and what is it going to do to ease the emigration of the Jews out of the Soviet Union?"

I have the written minutes of that debate here and just for illustration would like to quote a few statements. Our foreign minister admitted during the debate, "There are a lot of dependable reports of harassment in various ways to the minority Jewish population by the Soviet government agencies. Very often, people who are teaching or learning Hebrew are being questioned, their homes searched, and literature confiscated. Also, the number of emigration permits for Soviet Jews has been drastically reduced in recent months. Persons who apply for emigration permits have been very often exposed to heavy harassment."

The representative, Bonnie Bernstrom, explained further, "As the situation of the Jews in the Soviet Union in recent days has taken a turn for the worse, it would be correct to call it a threatening catastrophe. There are now 380,000 Jews in the Soviet Union waiting for an emigration visa to go to Israel. If someone applies for a visa he is being labeled a national traitor. In February of this year (1982) only 200 visas have been issued. This is only five percent in comparison to 1979. When a Jew applies for a visa, he loses his job and suddenly finds great difficulty in securing even the basic necessities of life. He also is risking being considered a parasite. Many are being tried before a court for anti-Soviet actions.

"The Jews do not have the possibility of perpetuating their own culture. They cannot issue any newspaper or magazine in Hebrew. They are not allowed to study Hebrew. In 1940 100,000 students went to Jewish schools and today the schools are almost non-existent.* The

---

*Any schools that may exist today probably would be unofficial and held secretly in homes.

number of synagogues shrank from 450 to 65. And now there are only 57* synagogues. There are two rabbis for two million Jews in the Soviet Union. The Soviet Union represses the Jews in two ways: They are not permitted to live like Jews while living there, and they are not permitted to leave the country."

The representative Gabriel Romanus, who has been together with several Jews in Russia, reported, "I had the opportunity to meet some of them (Jews) who were living outside of society. They had applied for an emigration visa and it had been denied. While in contact with these people, I saw the evidence that despite their tragic background, there was an unwillingness to bow and an unbroken desire for liberty. It is something I shall never forget. I saw evidence of the importance of staying together and of being independent in difficult material situations."

Professor Alexander Lerna told me during our conversation, "The last nine years after I applied for an emigration visa have been the best years of my life, despite harassment, despite the fact that I lost my work, my position, and duties. During these years," he said, "I was able to live an honest life and I was free from all hypocrisy, which is a normal way of life in the communistic Soviet society."

This debate in the Parliament was an answer to

---

*Estimates vary on the number of synagogues from 45 to 65, depending on who reports the figures and when they are reported.

the prayers of our prayer groups that our government would recognize the issue of the Soviet Jews. We were very thankful that the problem had been discussed on the government level. Representatives of all parties participated with the exception of the Communist party. They all agreed about the difficult situation of the Jews in the Soviet Union, and that the Swedish people will have to do something for the Jews there. The foreign minister made the last statement, "What can Sweden do, to make bearable the conditions of the Soviet Jews? We can contribute to international opinion. If we don't raise our voice, we don't know who else will do so. We can raise issues like we have done during the debate.

"We can condemn persecution. We can request that the Soviet Union live up to the international human requirements of the Treaty of Helsinki, the guidelines of the United Nations, and several other documents!"

Eberhard: Rev. Sjoberg, thank you very much for this conversation and your view of the situation in Sweden.

CHAPTER 12

DENMARK

Compiled by Eberhard Muehlan

In Denmark I met Christians, just as I did in Finland and Sweden, who testified that some time ago the Lord had put the burden for Jews in the Soviet Union on their hearts. They had been led to pray and begin some practical preparations. Some have prepared their homes for visitors and set up food and clothing storage. Some keep their summer homes ready, others have extended rooms or built additions to their farm houses.

Of all the reports, the one of a Danish missionary lady impressed me the most. It is one example out of many others.

"Even as a young girl, the Lord had put a deep love into my heart for and a desire to minister to the Jews. It was surely a determining factor that I got my nurse's training at a Jewish Orthodox hospital in London. With this training, I wanted to serve God on the mission field.

"I went to live in Indonesia. I still remember God speaking to me in the year of 1972, 'Your time here will come to an end; prepare for your departure!' At first I was shocked, but in my heart I knew that it was right. Where was I supposed to go? Should I begin to learn a new language? 'Go back to Europe!' went through my mind.

"Spontaneously it slipped out of me, 'How fortunate! That way I will be able to refresh some of the languages I already know.'

" 'Brush up your German!' the Lord said to me. I did not like that at all.

" 'After all, I am Danish and You expect me to go to Germany? Look at all the things that the Germans have committed in my country in the past. That's where You tell me I must go?' Because of all my rebellion, no answer came from the Lord. It was only after I gave up my resistance that I got the next direction.

" 'Minister unto My beloved people, the Jews in eastern Europe!'

"Seven years went by after this conversation with the Lord. I experienced one of the greatest difficulties in Indonesia during the civil war of the natives. I lost all my belongings and was confronted with a seemingly hopeless refugee situation. I also saw how the anti-Semitic* propaganda in Indonesia turned worse and worse. But I felt God's leading and protecting hand over me.

"My mind was occupied with the questions about the end times and God's prophecies concerning His people in that period of time. During my Bible studies and my prayers, it became clear to me that God will indeed lead His people soon out of 'the land of the north.'

"In 1979 I knew that my time in Indonesia had come to an end and I was to go back to Europe. At first I went back to Denmark and studied everything about the Jews that I could get my hands on.

"Up to that time I had never met anybody with whom I could share my burden about the exodus of the Jews from eastern Europe. I thought that I was the only one with this knowledge and I said to myself, 'If this is of the Lord, then there must be other people who can give me a confirmation.'

"It was in the spring of 1980 that a messianic Jew in Paris confided in me that he had received the same thoughts from God. A few months later the spokesman for the International Christian Embassy in Jerusalem, Jan Willem van der Hoeven, spoke in Denmark. After the meeting I worked up enough courage to go to him and share my impressions. He again confirmed to me that the Lord had given the same message to many people in different countries, but that I was the first one in Denmark who had told him about it.

"Then I knew that the burden I have had in my heart for years was really of the Lord. I was so glad

---

*Anti-Semitism is prejudice, discrimination against, or persecution of the Jewish people.

that He had spoken to many people and now I began to share boldly that which God had matured in my heart over the years — that the Soviet Jews would come via Finland to Denmark and move on via Holland to Israel. With this event, the great war of Gog and Magog, which Ezekiel 39 describes, must be very close.

"I first worked with refugees in Denmark and then for some time with immigrating Soviet Jews in Vienna. I traveled several times in the Soviet Union and shared the message of the exodus of the Jews. In 1982 the Lord led me to Israel to work from there in preparation to receive the Jews from the Soviet Union. Here I meet many people with the same burden. One of them has been Steve Lightle. We are all part of God's plan to bring about the realization of His promises in the Old Testament. God knows how to prepare each of us for that special place in His plan."

In a small village in the north of Denmark there is an older couple who own a Bible and recreation center and a former dairy. They claim that God told them to remodel the two buildings and later learned that it would be for the benefit of the Russian Jews that would be coming by their property. They now can shelter more than 200 people in the two buildings that they have remodeled.

This is their story that they sent to me by cassette tape. A friend of mine has visited them and verified the story;

"In September, 1976, we found it was necessary for my husband to stay in a hospital for a longer period of time than we had expected, due to a severe illness. In time he became more and more depressed because there seemed to be no improvement in his health. I was, of course, greatly concerned about him.

"But one day when I came to visit him, he was full of joy and excitement. 'I must talk to you alone,' he said. 'What I have experienced is so fantastic that you should not tell anybody about it yet.' Excitedly he told me how the Lord had come to his hospital room. 'I felt like I was lifted up in the air,' he explained, 'and then I heard two voices behind me. One said comfortingly, "Be still, be still!" And the other said, "You and your wife have difficult times, but I will use you. One day you will have a big house in a small village and serve Me, surrounded by other Christians. You will have to endure many hard times in the future but I will be with you all the time." '

"My husband's face glowed when he told me about this experience. I could see that he had gained new strength for his life.

"When he was dismissed from the hospital, difficult times did come. For twenty-five years we had owned our own business. But because of my husband's long illness, the profits had diminished. Finally, in 1980, we had to sell the business. But we held on to the word that the Lord had spoken to my husband. We knew the Lord wanted to use us!

"We started to work for the Lord wherever there was something to do. Soon the doors opened for us to take over a Bible and recreation center. Then in 1981 the dairy on the opposite side of the street was offered to us. We felt the leading of the Lord to buy it and remodel it to accommodate many people, even without knowing for sure what we would do with that many rooms.

"Then one of our guests told us about a vision he had seen while staying with us. 'In the vision,' he said, 'I saw people with small bundles under their arms coming to your place. You opened your doors and said, "Come in, we have lots of rooms." And that was it,' he explained. Well, we had just purchased and remodeled the big building across the street and had lots of rooms.

"Two years later a lady, who was spending her holidays with us, came to us and said, 'Last night I had a vision. I saw many men, women, and children. They came up the road from the south to your two buildings. You opened the door and said, "Come in, we have lots of rooms." '

"We were quite surprised. Here, two years later, we were hearing the same vision described by another person. But we still didn't know what it was all about.

"Some time later we got a letter from a lady in Copenhagen. She told us that the Lord had put it on her heart to tell us that we should be ready to take in many refugees, especially Jews. This letter confirmed again what we had heard through the visions of the other two people.

"We knew that between the two major buildings we had enough room to potentially house 200 people. But, we wondered where we would get the means to furnish so many rooms. Without taking any initiative on our own, the Lord started to work. People began to give us things like beds, sheets, blankets, used clothing, and money. Now we are prepared to house up to 200 people at a time.

"Another concern that we had was that we are both in our fifties and we are aware that our energy and time will only stretch so far. We would definitely need help in order to take care of such a large place and to serve so many people. What a joy it was when a young couple moved in to help us. They had heard God's call to help and were obedient to come and be available.

"After Steve Lightle had spoken in Denmark, many of our friends from different parts of the country phoned and asked, 'Don't you think that this is the ministry for which God has been preparing you?' But we couldn't imagine taking in Russian Jews because we hadn't ever heard anything about the possibility that God would bring the Jewish people out of Russia.

"Then, we listened to Steve's cassette tape. Obviously the Lord had been trying since 1976 to prepare us step by step to be of assistance in His plan.

"There was just one other question that I had often pondered. 'How can we take in Russian Jews without knowing one word of their language?' When I shared my concern with the young couple who assist us, the husband enthusiastically said, 'Oh, my mother speaks seven languages fluently, and among them is Russian.'

"This lady is now planning to move into our center and through her we will be able to communicate with the Russian Jews when they come.

"The Lord has spoken so clearly to us, enabled us to be equipped and prepared, and has given us so many confirmations that we are full of expectation.

We are confident that God will be bringing lots of Russian Jewish refugees our way."

CHAPTER 13

THE NETHERLANDS

Compiled by Eberhard Muehlan

In Holland I once again saw the same picture as in all the other countries I had been visiting. I was able to get together with Christians to whom God had spoken that He would get His people out of the Soviet Union, and that the Dutch people had the commission to receive them. The personal life stories and leadings of every person I met made a deep impression on me.

At first I visited two ladies who, together, have been managing an old age home for many years. As they were praying together in 1977, they heard God speak the first time about the Soviet Jews. The thought that came to their mind during prayer was, "This house is for My people as they come out of the East."* Never, ever, had they heard anything like

---

*In this chapter the Russian Jews are referred to as being "from the East," referring to the eastern Communist block countries behind the Iron Curtain. These countries are east of Holland, but in relationship to Israel, they are to the "north."

this from someone else. It was completely new to them.

Then came more directions. One of the ladies, who spoke German, reported to me, "In February of 1978, God made it clear to me that I was to learn Russian and Arabic. We had seen in our vision that we were nursing sick Jews from the East in our house. Both of us are hospital nurses and we believe that we will take in those sick Jews and care for them.

"Later on, God showed us how to prepare in practical ways. Normally we could accommodate fifteen people, but if the need arises we can now make space for thirty to fifty people. We have beds and blankets, all medication in storage that a small hospital might need, and enough food supply for three months.

"We figure that the Lord will make sure that the house will be empty during the time it is needed. That is the reason we are not taking in anybody now. Last summer our last resident guest died. Our home is prepared. Presently we are just having the office of a Christian organization in the house. We spend many hours in prayer and are always ready to have guests.

"In 1978, we had to sell the house next to our present property. We took it as a sign from God that a medical doctor purchased the place. He is a Jew from Poland who speaks Polish, Hebrew, and seven Russian dialects. We have become very good friends.

"Surely we have had some doubts since we did not know anybody who had the same calling and we really felt all alone. It was only two years ago that we became acquainted with other Christians from Holland who had heard the same thing from God and it was good to be able to share with each other. We got to know Steve Lightle just last year and his message was also a tremendous confirmation for us."

Another couple I met in the Netherlands had converted a former monastery into a retreat and counseling center in 1974. Their project was very interesting as it always is when people put their lives and everything they have into the hands of God. This type of commitment is always the prerequisite for experiencing God's care and guidance. These people are totally committed.

Their property includes several buildings, a greenhouse, and thirty-four acres of farmland. As they began their work, somebody shared with them a vision and a Bible verse which influenced their future calling. The person had seen a star with many points over their property and written in the center of it was Isaiah 4:1-6. The last verse of the six verses especially spoke to them, *"And there will be a shelter to give shade from the heat by day, and refuge and protection from storm and the rain."*

The wife reported, "I said to myself, the real purpose of the Lord for our lives will not be to operate a recreation and counseling center. With this fantastic piece of property, He has greater things in store. God made it clear to us to prepare ourselves to help people in need, perhaps refugees who because of military conflicts, are looking for a place of refuge in Holland. It didn't occur to me that these could be Jews.

"But you know, just yesterday I received a cassette of Steve Lightle from a friend in Germany with the message that the Jews shall come out of the

Soviet Union. Actually I did not think that I had time to listen to it, but because I did not feel well, I lay down on the sofa and listened to the cassette. Then I again had to read the verses in Isaiah 4 that God had given us at the start of our ministry. I noticed something that had always been there, but that over the years we had hardly paid any attention to. The text refers to 'the branch of the Lord,' and 'the survivors of Israel,' 'Zion,' and 'Jerusalem.' This distinctly describes the children of Israel, for whom we shall be a shelter to give shade and a place of refuge from the storm. What God has been speaking to us over the past years is now clearer for us."

Here I was sitting with these wonderful Christians and it was not necessary for me to explain things to them. Our Heavenly Father had made this wonderful arrangement, that exactly one day before my visit, they received Steve's cassette so that their calling could be confirmed and become clear to them.

Since 1977, a group of Catholic Christians have been living in a beautiful old castle doing recreational and counseling work. How they received this castle is an exciting story in itself of the Lord's guidance. The director shared some personal things with me. "Since my early youth," he said, "I have had love for the Jewish people. Perhaps it was because of all the events of World War II that I felt in my heart an obligation to help these people. So when I began the work at the castle, I had the vague idea in the back of my mind that in the future we would be able to do something for the Jews.

"At one of our prayer meetings with all the

workers, I had this short word from the Lord, 'Some day you will cook kosher food in your kitchen!' I shared it with the others but did not know what to do with it. Later at a Bible seminar, the guest speaker had a vision of me. He saw me in the castle. The lower rooms were all filled with beds and mattresses. He saw that I was walking down the hall and tending to the people. I cannot forget that he pointed out that these people did not have faces like western Europeans, but that their profiles and skin coloring were more like the people we know from eastern Europe. As we have been able to share with other Christians about the guidance we have received concerning the exodus of the Jews from the Soviet Union via Holland, the vision has become quite clear. We want to be obedient and are prepared to help these people."

I took some time to talk with a man who is a member of the "Intercessors for Holland." He is constantly traveling to hold weekend prayer meetings and to counsel in Holland. He said that recently more and more people have been coming to him to share how God has shown them the responsibility Holland has toward the Jews who will be coming out of the East.

"Wherever I have spoken in the last few months," he said, "people have come up to me and shared something about the matter. In a way it was kind of funny, because every person thought that he or she was the only one to whom God had spoken. But in actuality, there have been many. I myself was made aware of the subject in 1979 while I was reading through the book of the prophet Jeremiah. The thought occurred to me, 'Many things will have to take place. There are only a comparatively few Jews in Israel now.' After that, I met more and more people who had had the same thought.

"I remember one prayer weekend when God had put on our hearts all day, 'Pray for Israel.' At another time in one particular coastal town we had the burden to pray that the Jews would be received willingly in that city and coastal area. One participant of that day of prayer reported later on that his daughter had had a dream at home while our evening prayer meeting was going on. She saw how ships with Jewish refugees aboard came across the sea and into the harbor of that little town. She described the meadows, the coastline, the waters, and a street sign with the name of the town we had been praying for. Even though she had never been to that town, from her dream she could describe everything exactly the way things are in reality!"

In another conversation, this man testified that he personally knows at least fifty people in Holland to whom God had spoken about the exodus of the Jews from the Soviet Union. "Most of them have received the inspiration from God without knowing one another," he said. "At first I thought these people were imagining things, but as I met more and more Christians who testified the same thing I knew that this must be from God. I know the owner of a hotel with eighty beds. The man is a Christian and when he heard about the predicted exodus of the Jews, he offered to help immediately. Quite a number of Christians have stored away groceries. I know of a huge clothing warehouse where just recently clothing valued at 18,000 guilders ($7,200) has been stored up. More and more Christians are open to help when the exodus occurs."

A medical doctor explained to me how he had received his instructions from God. For quite some time he had been interested in the Jewish people and then he read in the Bible that all the Jews will eventually return to Israel, especially those out of Russia. In a prayer meeting in 1981, he began to pray for the Jews in Russia, and he saw in a vision a geographical map of Europe. Many parts of Germany were filled with darkness, but in the north it showed a white path clear across Germany on which the Jews will move toward Holland. Up to that day he had never heard anything like it. He concluded that he and the rest of the people in this prayer group should prepare themselves to receive Jewish refugees. After that he met other Christians with the same burden. As a result of this, they have formed a Christian organization for the purpose of preparing Christians spiritually and practically for difficult times. They believe this will include helping the Jewish refugees from Russia.

"I myself am under the impression that the Jews will come at a time of great difficulty," he explained to me. "Others in our group believe that after the exodus of the Jews, military conflicts could follow. That's why we have to be prepared and we see our calling in this: to give spiritual and practical guidance on how to be strong in difficult times and to be able to help others."

It was especially interesting to me to meet with

people who had received God's instruction to pray for the border between Holland and Germany. These Christians had also heard from God that Jews will move through Germany into Holland. They are praying for uninterrupted travel across the border.

One of them told me, "It was about the end of 1981 that our prayer group began to intercede for our country. It was then the Spirit of God made it clear to us that we should pray for the border, that the Jews would be able to cross freely. We had clear direction to pray for a section of the border of about thirty-six miles long right in our vicinity. For three to four months we drove every Monday to the border and prayed for the section that God had told us to pray for.

"Later on, we got to know another prayer group who had also received the calling to pray for the border. We asked them if God had told them to pray for a certain section of the border. We found out that they had been praying for the section just north of ours. Then we found out that there is a prayer group who has been praying for the border just south of us. Altogether now I know four prayer groups who have independently received direction from God to pray for the Dutch-German border, without originally having any knowledge of each other."

CHAPTER 14

GERMANY

Compiled by Eberhard Muehlan

Impressed with all the testimonies, I returned home and asked myself, "How do all these preparations compare with what is happening in Germany?" Up to this point I had not been able to collect very many reports from Germany. I had come to understand that those to whom God has spoken have typically had great reservations about sharing their knowledge with others. However, I was sure that God had been speaking to many people in Germany as well, and in the last few weeks, I have been able to discover some of these.

For example, there was the young lady who handed me a letter at a meeting in which she wrote that God had shown her in May 1980 to go to Israel. Some time later, another Christian gave her a word from the Lord, saying that some day she would be helping people who are refugees and in great need. Other people testified to her that these refugees would be Jews and that God wanted to use her to help them. When she heard me speak on this subject at the meeting, it was a further confirmation to her.

Many people told me that in the last few years they had been able to buy or build a larger house than they had intended. While at one time they had questioned why, they now knew that they had the answer.

The reports of individual Christians who have had a revelation of the coming final exodus of the Jews out of the Soviet Union are increasing. Now, as the message becomes more widely known, there is also a clearer picture and the public knowledge of God's plan and direction increases.

In January of 1983, Steve Lightle was in Berlin for a few days holding meetings. One Christian came up and told him that he had 4,000 Russian Bibles at his house that he wanted to give to the people at the meeting. So, he went home and got the 4,000 Bibles and distributed them so that the believers could have them on hand when the Jews come through Berlin on their way west.

While Steve and the man who distributed the Bibles were having breakfast the next day, a question arose. How can the Christians effectively give the Russian Bibles as a personal gift since most of them do not speak that language? After pondering the problem for awhile, they came up with the idea of inserting a letter into each Bible. The letter will include a personal note and a welcome. Steve dictated the letter to the man in English and by the next day, they had the letter translated into Russian and Hebrew and printed back to back. This is the letter, along with the English translation:

Мой дорогой еврейский друг!

Уже много лет мы знаем из Священного Писания, что ты приедешь в эту страну.

Мы любим тебя и хотели-бы, чтобы ты знал, что мы также любим Бога Израиля.

Поэтому наши сердца, также как и двери наших домов всегда открыты для тебя.

Да будет с вами Божье благословение, вы так много перенесли.

Мы желаем тебе мужества в деле возвращения на землю предков, как это часто упоминается в слове Божьем Ер. 23,7-8; 31,7-9; Ис. 11:11; 43:5-6; 43:11 Ты также воплощение этих предсказаний.

И также, как в старые времена Господь заключил союз по выходу наших предков из Египта также Он хочет иметь этот союз с тобой в наши дни.

Прими пожалуйста Библию, нашу любовь и полюбишь, чтобы она была твоей неразлучной спутницей, при возвращении в страну наших отцов - Авраама, Исаака и Иакова.

Господь Бог исполнил каждое данное слово из Библии и сегодня Он сдерживает свое слово для тебя, потому что Он тебя любит.

4-Моисей - 6; 24-26

Да будет с тобой помощь и благословение Господа!
Да призрит на тебя Господь светлым лицом Своим и помилует тебя!
Да обратит Господь лицо Свое на тебя и даст тебе мир!

חברי היקרים!

יודעים אנו זה כבר שנים שאתם
תצברו דרך הארץ הזאת, ככתוב
בתנ"ך. באהבתנו הגדולה אליכם
רוצים אנו שתדעו כי גם לנו אותה
האהבה לה' אלהי ישראל. לכן פתחנו
את לבנו ואת בתנו לכם.
ברצוננו לבך אתכם כי ידוע לנו
כמה שסבלתם. תקותנו הגדולה היא
שיום אחד תחזרו לארצכם כפי שאמר
ה' לנביא ירמיהו בפסוקים הבאים

ירמיה	7+8 :	23	כג
	7-9 :	31	לא
ישעיה	11 :	11	יא
	5+6 :	43	מג
	16-19 :	43	מג

אתם תגשימו את הנבואה הזאת כפי
שהאל הקים את בריתו עם אברהם
כתן תורתו בהר סיני. גם צמכם
רוצה האל להקים ברית בכדי
שתקחו את התורה לאהבה. אנו מתן
את עזרתנו בהיותכם בדרך לארצכם
שהובטחה לאבותיכם. האל קיים את דברו
כתוב בתורתו, והיום ה' ממשיך לקיים
את דברו באהבתו הרבה.

יברכך ה' וישמרך: יאר ה' פניו אליך ויחנך
שא ה' פניו אליך וישם לך שלום (6 : 24-26 ובמדבר)

My dear Jewish friend:

We welcome you from the bottom of our hearts! For many years we have known from the Holy Spirit that you would come through our country. We love you and want you to know that we also love the God of Israel. Therefore, our hearts and the doors of our homes are open for you. You have suffered much, but may the grace of God abide in your life.

We wish you much courage for your return into the land of your forefathers. Your return had been promised in the Word of God: Jeremiah 23:7,8; 31:7-9; Isaiah 11:11; 43:5-6, 16-19. You are a part of the fulfillment of these promises! As the Lord God has kept His covenant in former times with your ancestors by leading them out of Egypt, so He wants to stand by your side as you are being led forth now.

Please take this Bible as a sign of our love and help. May this book get your undivided attention on your way back into the land of your father Abraham, Isaac, and Jacob.

Our God has kept all of His promises in the Bible up to now. He will also fulfill the promises of your homecoming, because He loves you!

The LORD bless you, and keep you; the

LORD make his face shine upon you, and be
gracious to you; the LORD lift up His
countenance on you, and give you peace!
(Numbers 6:24-26).

Through some unusual circumstances, more than
200,000 Russian Bibles are available that had been
originally destined to be smuggled into the Soviet
Union. These Russian Bibles are now on their way to
Berlin where the Russian/Hebrew letter will be in-
serted. While some of those Bibles may still reach the
Soviet Union, the remainder will be stored in Berlin,
ready for the final exodus of the Jews.

In Berlin, I met a lady who told me about a very
impressive experience. She had moved to Israel in
November of 1980 to live with some other Christians.
During a prayer meeting in the spring of 1981, she
saw herself in a vision, standing in Germany to
welcome many Russian Jews and to lead them via
Naples, Italy, on to Israel. A week later, in the same
prayer group, she had the same vision, but the Lord
added these words, "You will walk with a cloud during the day and a pillar of fire by night."

She explained to me, "Normally we share with
our group what God says to each of us individually. In
this way, the picture of God's will for our group
becomes clearer. We share and try to discern the
validity of each thing in order to be sure of what God
has been saying. But this time I hesitated to share the
new portion of the vision because I thought it could
not possibly pertain to me. Not even three minutes

passed when a sister from Australia began to prophesy and said, among other things, 'You will move
with a cloud during the day and a pillar of fire by
night.' Praise the Lord! He knows how to remove our
doubts!

"I moved from Israel back to Germany. Then the
Lord pointed out to me that the Russian Jews will
come to western Germany through Berlin. He asked
me to pray that the hearts of the Russian Jews would
be prepared for their exodus. The words of the Lord
to me were to build a highway of prayer in the city of
Berlin. Now I know why the Lord had me move to
Berlin.

"Then for the first time in January of 1983, I
heard Steve Lightle as he gave the message concerning the Jewish exodus. While listening to him, I found
complete agreement and confirmation with what the
Lord had shown to me independently."

People may ask, "What is happening in
Braunschweig, the city where Steve Lightle first
heard from God on this subject? According to God's
revelation to Steve, the people of this city will have,
next to Berlin, one of the greatest challenges as the
Jews move through it."

I know quite a few people in and around
Braunschweig who feel God's call to prayer and to be
prepared to help. Many hearts and homes are open for
the Jews to come. For instance, a family who must
move to a different area of Braunschweig are very
sure that they must not take just any house, but a
large house out in the country with lots of room and
property. That way they will be able to provide hous-

ing for the Jewish refugees.

A young and committed church fellowship in Braunschweig recently purchased a building complex that an outsider might say is several sizes too big for that group of Christians. Actually there is about 15,000 square feet of space that is not presently needed. While the church has plans for possible use of these rooms for various purposes for the fellowship, the layout of the complex permits quick changes in order to accommodate the Jews.

Interestingly enough, this church started a car repair shop. The primary goal is to repair the cars of the church members and to give the young people a place to learn a profession in this time of increasing unemployment. But they also feel that the shop will be used to quickly and inexpensively repair cars for the transportation of the Jews. On top of that, there are people in the church who have begun to learn Russian.

Not far away from Braunschweig, there is a Bible school that accommodates 160 beds. There is also a lot of storage area and plenty of property. They are prepared for the possibility of housing many people in a moment's notice. However, more importantly, this Bible school is a fortress of prayer. All staff members and students know how to pray effectively and to battle spiritually on behalf of the persecuted Christians and Jews in the Soviet Union.

I found an additional independent witness of the prophetic revelations of God in Arie Ben Israel, a messianic Jew. He was born in a concentration camp in Siberia, where his parents were committed to nine years of hard labor. Later, at their release in 1960, they immigrated to Israel. While visiting Germany in the year of 1975, Arie received Jesus as his personal Messiah. Since 1976, he has lived in Bad Nauheim, West Germany. He has a ministry of reconciliation between the Jews and the Germans, and also among the denominations.

Arie testified to me that God had been speaking to him for three years that the Lord would lead the Jews out of the Soviet Union. In a vision, he saw on various maps how the Jews were gathering in the Soviet Union. Some came via Berlin to West Germany. Others came over the Finnish border to freedom. But God had also told him not to talk about it, since His plans would have to mature and that preparation was needed through prayer and fasting.

At the end of 1982, God gave Arie liberty to share this vision at a conference. After the meeting, a man came up to him and asked if he had ever heard Steve Lightle's message on the final exodus of the Jews.

"No," Arie said. "Up to this point, I had been under the impression that I was the only one to whom God had ever spoken about this. Before this, I have never heard anyone else talk about it."

Later, when I personally interviewed Arie, he said, "When Steve Lightle contacted me in January of 1983, we were happy to find that we were in unison about what God had shown each of us."

CHAPTER 15

ACTION AROUND THE WORLD

Compiled by Eberhard Muehlan

Up to now, all my writing has been limited to the testimonies from Europe. However, at this point I would like to make it known that God has also spoken to many people around the world about His plan to bring His people home to Israel.

I met a Christian woman from Japan who told me that she had heard about the exodus of the Jews out of Russia more than ten years ago. Her pastor in Japan had received a word from the Lord on the matter. From the pulpit he told his congregation, "The Lord revealed to me that the Jews in the Soviet Union will move back to their homeland via Europe." Since that time, this church has been praying for this to come to pass.

This woman was really excited when she heard Steve Lightle speak. What he shared confirmed what she had heard from her pastor so many years ago.

Pastor Ralph Rutledge, of the Queensway

Cathedral in Toronto, Canada, received God's leading to call his congregation to a forty-day fast. *"Blow a trumpet in Zion, consecrate a fast, proclaim a solemn assembly"* (Joel 2:15). So he challenged all 2,000 members of his church to begin the new year (1983) with fasting and prayer, beginning with the month of January. His church has not been the same since that event!

On January 23, about halfway through the fast, the assistant pastor, Clyde Williamson, received the following prophecy:

"The Spirit of God is wooing people to do that which Queen Esther did in an absolute fast unto God. He shall give an appointed time, and there shall be those that shall set themselves aside without food and drink for a period of three days. God will take His people out of bondage from all over the globe. They shall come forth by the thousands and by the millions and His name shall be lifted up in their midst."

Immediately, Queensway Cathedral sent a "Decree for an Esther Fast" throughout the world proclaiming that Christians everywhere should fast and pray especially for the freedom of the Jews in the Soviet Union.

We know from the Bible that Queen Esther called for a three-day total fast when she was warned by her uncle Mordecai of the plan for complete destruction of her Jewish people there in Persia. Backed by the prayers of the Jews across that nation, Esther was able to be the tool in God's hand to save the Jews from the terrible annihilation plans of Haman.

Similarly, just as these Jews fasted and prayed and were delivered, so Christians all around the world were challenged to fast during the 1983 Easter season for the return of Jewish people to their homeland, especially those who are in bondage in Russia.

The Esther Fast Decree that went around the world is reproduced on the next page.

Thousands of Christians from many nations responded to this decree and committed themselves to the three-day fast. The church in Toronto received 17,000 pledges from all over the world. Thousands of others who did not take the time to sign a written pledge also joined the worldwide band of intercessors. Participants included people from such diverse places as the United States, Nigeria, and Mexico. Pastors like Yonggi Cho in Seoul, Korea and Volkhard Spitzer in West Berlin, West Germany and their congregations supported the Esther Fast.

Pastor Rutledge reported, "I have met with some of the leading rabbis regarding this fast, and they have been deeply moved by our sincere desire to see God's Word fulfilled in them as His ancient people."

The prophet Isaiah has given some clear directions and reasons for such a fast:

> *"Is this not the fast which I choose,*
> *To loosen the bonds of wickedness,*
> *To undo the bands of the yoke,*
> *And to let the oppressed go free,*
> *And break every yoke?"* (Isaiah 58:6)

A Decree From The Lord

THE ESTHER FAST

Decreed For
April 1st, 2nd and 3rd, 1983

The Purpose Of This Call To Fast And Pray:

That believers everywhere throughout the globe request from God the return of His ancient people Israel to their homeland.

- To pray for their release from bondage.
- To witness the lifting of the name of the Lord in the midst of Israel.
- To see Israel set free in spirit to fulfill her mission and commission which has been commanded in Holy Scripture.

Isaiah 52: 5-10 (KJV)

5. Now therefore, what have I here, saith the Lord, that my people is taken away for nought? they that rule over them make them to howl, saith the Lord; and my name continually every day is blasphemed.

6. Therefore my people shall know my name: therefore they shall know in that day that I am he that doth speak: behold, it is I.

7. How beautiful upon the mountains are the feet of him that bringeth good tidings, that publisheth peace; that bringeth good tidings of good, that publisheth salvation; that saith unto Zion, Thy God reigneth!

8. Thy watchmen shall lift up the voice; with the voice together shall they sing: for they shall see eye to eye, when the Lord shall bring again Zion.

8. The watchmen shout and sing with joy, for right before their eyes they see the Lord God bring His people home again. (Living Bible)

9. Break forth into joy, sing together, ye waste places of Jerusalem: for the Lord hath comforted his people, he hath redeemed Jerusalem.

10. The Lord hath made bare his holy arm in the eyes of all the nations; and all the ends of the earth shall see the salvation of our God.

- To see the Church of Jesus Christ brought into her fullest liberty to be a mighty voice in all the earth.

The Type of Fast Declared . . . Esther 4:16 (NIV)

"Do not eat or drink for three days, night or day" This decreed fast is for the first three days of April which falls on the Easter weekend, precisely in the middle of the Jewish passover week. The Passover speaks of Israel's deliverance from bondage.

Who May Participate?

All God's people who sense the liberty and calling to be part of this world wide absolute fast may participate. It is suggested that two exceptions be made only, for partaking in Holy Communion or for health reasons during these three days.

This is a call to fervent prayer placed upon the hearts of Canadians. It is a challenge to every believer around the world to break forth in great intercession for the greatest worldwide move of God's Holy Spirit ever known to mankind. Such came forth in the midst of a forty day fast Sunday evening January 23rd, 1983 in Toronto, Canada.

The Queensway Cathedral of Toronto, Canada gives permission to reprint and distribute this decree as is. Telephone: (416) 255-0141.

A "grass roots" organization has developed that is having an impact around the world in getting people informed about the plight of the Jews in the Soviet Union. Formed in September 1980 and called the "International Christian Embassy Jerusalem" (ICEJ), their motto is Isaiah 40:1: " 'Comfort, O comfort My People,' says your God."

In addition to their headquarters in Jerusalem, offices are located in five continents of the world. Their goal is to challenge Christians around the world to pray for and support Israel and the Jewish people, especially in the Soviet Union.

Six months after the founding of the Embassy, the "Mordecai Outcry" program was launched to express their ongoing, deep concern for the Soviet Jews. The name was taken from the book of Esther in the Old Testament because the desperate situation of the Russian Jews today is so similar to those of the Jews in Persia in Mordecai's time. Like Mordecai who lifted up his voice on behalf of God's people, so the "Christian Embassy" has vowed to constantly point out to the world the desperate situation of the Jews in the Soviet Union.

The first "Mordecai Outcry" sponsored by the Christian Embassy took place in 1981 at Passover time, when approximately 200 Christians met at Prime Minister Menachem Begin's office in Jerusalem. He was overwhelmed with the love and support he saw for his people. Soberly, he said, "Many of my own people judge me for seeing the return of the Jews to our land as a fulfillment of the prophets." He paused and said, "I plead guilty."

Here is the "Mordecai Outcry" statement that was proclaimed that day and then sent to the Soviet government officials:

"Soviet Union: This day in Jerusalem we speak out to you in the name of concerned Christians throughout the world. We urge you to release all Jews who want to leave your country. We appeal to you to be human, human enough to give freedom to all Prisoners of Zion who are suffering at your hands.

"We are especially concerned about the fate of prisoners such as Anatoly Scharansky, Vladimir Slepak, Ida Nudel, Josef Begun, and others whose health is deteriorating to the point where their lives are in danger. We are also distressed because many Christians are also being persecuted in your country.

"For over fifty years, millions of people have met their death in concentration camps all over the Soviet Union. Multitudes have been tortured physically, mentally, and spiritually. At this moment, you are torturing Jews simply because they have requested visas to leave your country. This is appalling to all civilized people everywhere!

"We declare to you that God sees the anguish and hears the torment of His people. He has laid it upon our hearts to solemnly warn you that His Word makes it clear, as in the days of Pharaoh, He will call you to judgment if you stubbornly refuse His command to "LET MY PEOPLE GO!"

"Our cry this day began in Jerusalem and it will be taken up by Christians everywhere. We will keep crying out in major capitals of the world until you set these people free. Let the Soviet Jews go free! Let Anatoly Scharansky go free! Set all Prisoners of Zion free!"

Johann Luckhoff, who is from South Africa and now the Director of the International Christian Embassy Jerusalem, emphasized that the "Mordecai Outcry" was not a one-time demontration. "It is a model to be taken up by Christians in the major capitals of the world," he said, "until the Lord fulfills His promise of the greatest exodus of all, foretold by Jeremiah in chapter 23:7-8."

Similar "Mordecai Outcry" demonstrations took place all over the world in the fall of 1981. On November 13th, 1982, 2,000 Dutch Christians in The Hague met with members of the Parliament. Then they marched to the Soviet Embassy where they presented Soviet Embassy officials with a petition of protest that was co-signed by members of the Dutch Parliament.

The participants also gave the following press release to the Dutch newspapers for publication: "With growing concern we see that the same thing is happening to the Jews in Soviet Russia as was their lot in Nazi Germany on the eve of the Second World War. As in Germany, the Soviet Union is now able to continue with this oppression so long as she can keep it a secret and we, who are able to raise our voices, allow it. Because we do not want to belong to the majority whose silence made possible the holocaust of 1940-45, we feel compelled to raise our voices on behalf of all Jewish prisoners who are being mistreated because they want to make use of their right to leave the Soviet Union. They are being denied this legal right which is theirs according to the Helsinki Final Act of 1975, of which the Soviet Union is a signatory."

Jan Willem van der Hoeven, spokesman for the Embassy, addressed Christians and Knesset members at the March 16 "Mordecai Outcry" demonstration in Jerusalem. "God has been faithful in bringing the Jews from the four corners of the earth," he said, "from more than one hundred nations, to this wonderful land. That same God is also able to keep His promise to bring them out of the north. Concerned Christians throughout the world are also taking up the call going out of Jerusalem to 'Let My People Go'."

Van der Hoeven declared, "We are prepared to lift up our voices for the Jews in two ways. First and foremost, in prayer and fasting, which only underlines what we believe, that it is God and not ourselves who is going to bring this exodus to pass. And by the grace of God, we also will stand in front of the Soviet embassies around the world and promise, with God's help, not to keep silent again."

The demonstration was concluded with a bold statement by van der Hoeven to Yuri Andropov: "We are not here as beggars pleading, 'Please, Yuri Andropov, bring the Jews to us.' You may use the United Nations, you may use conferences, you may distract world opinion by pointing the finger at Israel with all of your venomous reporting. We Christians will not be fooled. If you want to keep us quiet, send the Jews home."

Prime Minister Begin expressed his deepest gratitude to the demonstrators for their strong stand on behalf of the Jewish people. Menachem Savidor, speaker of the Knesset, also thanked the Christians saying, "While many people are involved in castigating, berating, and slaughtering Israel, you came and gave us courage and world support."

In addition to media coverage in Israel, there were shortwave radio broadcasts to the people of the Soviet Union by Kol-Israel's Russian service and Voice of Hope, the Christian radio ministry in Southern Lebanon. Foreign journalists and radio broadcasters were present, and United Press International taped the entire demonstration and broadcast portions of it throughout the world.

Additional "Mordecai Outcry" demonstrations were staged before Soviet embassies in the United States, Canada, England, Ireland, France, the Netherlands, Sweden, Norway, Denmark, Germany, Switzerland, New Zealand, and Australia.

CHAPTER 16

EVALUATION OF THE FIELDTRIPS

Compiled by Eberhard Muehlan

The reader will surely have noticed that I have gone on my journeys with skepticism and have returned greatly impressed. I collected a lot of material but I have only reported a small percentage of it. I must also admit that I have met people whose reports seemed to me to be dubious. It would have been strange if, with such a prophetic theme as this, I would have found only credible testimonies. It always seems as though in this area there is special opportunity for the flesh to get in the way.

On the other hand, I am sure there are many more Christians than the ones that we were able to contact who have had revelations of the final exodus.

If you, as the reader, belong to that group to which God has spoken in the past concerning the situation of the Jews in the Soviet Union, then please receive this book as an encouragement that you have not been mistaken. You are not standing alone! You have become a part of God's redemptive plan with many others and you can be full of expectancy about what God will do through you in the future.

Some of the readers may not be used to expressions like "vision," or "prophecy," or sayings like, "God has told me." Even if the speaking of God personally today may be a completely new experience for some, it is definitely rooted in the Bible. Jesus Himself said, "My sheep hear My voice" (John 10:27). We also read that, "For all who are being led by the Spirit of God, these are the sons of God" (Romans 8:14). Naturally it is also our obligation to check out everything. "But examine everything carefully; hold fast to that which is good" (I Thessalonians 5:21).

It was also impressive that I found that many times God had spoken not only to special people, but to those that some might call "ordinary Christians." His message was given to people of every denomination, age, and social level. But one characteristic that I observed with everyone was that they all had an attitude that would say, "Lord, I give myself to You just as I am. Change me and do with me what You would like to do. I don't want to take my life into my own hands, I want You to direct my life. I want Your will to be done." These are the kind of people God can trust and use for His purposes and plans. He is revealing to them His great plan for the final exodus of His people.

In summary, the testimonies that I investigated can be divided into three groups. The first group are those who first heard the message of the Jewish exodus through Steve Lightle or someone else. They have checked the message out in the Bible and then sought the Lord's guidance about what they should do. I belong to that group.

The second group are those Christians to whom God has spoken in the past, preparing them, but perhaps they did not realize that it was concerning the Jews from the East. When they heard the message about the Jews coming out of the Soviet Union, then they knew what God's intention had been in speaking to them before. Quite often I met people like that. For example, the Jewish couple in Finland who had purchased the farm house with the impression that they should help people in need. Later on the wife had the vision of poorly dressed people coming out of the woods across the meadow looking for a place of refuge. After they had received Steve Lightle's message on cassette, they understood that it had been God's leading to prepare them to receive the Jews out of the Soviet Union. This is a typical example of "continued revelation."

The third group will probably be the testimonies that are the most convincing to the critical reader. It includes those who had never before heard anything about the Jewish exodus from anyone, but had independently received instruction from the Lord. Take for instance, the examples of Rev. Kjell Sjoberg in Sweden, the two ladies in the old age home in Holland, and Arie Ben Israel from Germany. For each of those, Steve Lightle's message was confirmation of what God had already revealed to them. These are classic examples of God's individual way of revelation.

If there is still some reason for someone to doubt the truth of these reports, the person should ask, "Can it be possible for fifty reliable Christians to all be mistaken?" These are people who did not know each other. They are from different countries, backgrounds, and denominations. Did they just imagine these things and yet they all happened to confirm each other? Or, is this vast array of God's prophetic revelation proof in itself?

I would like to call into remembrance one verse of the Bible in Amos 3:7, *"Surely the Lord God does nothing unless He reveals His secret counsel to His servants the prophets."* It does not say to a "single" prophet, but that God will give revelation to "many" prophets. And this is exactly the multiple revelation that we have in this particular situation.

It might also be of interest that several of those to whom God has spoken in the last few years, and who were not allowed to talk about it, were released from their silence at the end of 1982 or the beginning of 1983. Now they feel the liberty to speak freely about it in public in order to prepare both Christians and Jews for the upcoming events.. Remember the Christians in Sweden who, during 1982, widely and publicly proclaimed the news. There's the group in Holland who, at the end of 1982, knew that they should not be silent anymore. Also, Steve Lightle and Arie Ben Israel, independently of each other, received the instruction at the end of 1982 that the time of silence was over.

Some people may be rather surprised at how many practical preparations have been going on for years: people learning Russian, preparing housing facilities, buying buses, storing clothes, setting aside grain, raising "beef on the hoof"! Are these things necessary? Is this the right point in time for such practical preparations? Are they ahead of schedule?

During my visits, I kept asking myself the same questions. I came to no final conclusions. The answers must be left for the future to confirm.

But the Christians I met and interviewed left a very solid impression on me. They were not enthusiastic dreamers who thought of nothing else but preparing for the Jews, forgetting the great commission that Jesus gave to His followers. They knew that as believers they were to primarily share the good news of the Gospel in order to bring people into the Kingdom of God and to build up the Body of Christ. But on the other hand, they were also aware that they should not forget that God has His special plans for His Jewish people. They believe that they are called of God to work together with Him as He brings to pass His prophetic purposes and plans for His "chosen people."

The practical preparations that I saw were carefully and wisely planned:

Houses and buildings that have been remodeled to accommodate the Jewish refugees are now being used for Christian retreat centers, Bible schools, rehabilitation work, or other practical enterprises.

Buses purchased for the eventual transport of the Jews are now being used for Christian endeavors. They are not idle or rusting in isolated parking lots.

Clothes, if stored properly, can last for years.

And, those who are storing them are also making the clothes available to anyone who needs them now.

Grain can be stored for decades and is good insurance against possible "hard times" ahead.

The man who is raising "beef on the hoof" to feed the Jews is also building an investment as he multiplies his stock.

We must also keep in mind that the Jewish refugees will be in transit. They may only stay in a given place for a day or two, or a week, or a month, or whatever time is necessary. It is God's plan to draw His people to Israel, not relocate them in other places along the way. An old Jewish proverb says: "Give a Jew who is traveling to Zion enough on his way so that he is not starving, but nothing more, otherwise he will get his eyes off the goal."

We need to prepare just enough to provide the necessities for the Jews on their way "home." But remember that there will be millions of them emigrating from the Iron Curtain countries. It will take a lot of preparations to provide for so many people. Only the Holy Spirit can show each person what to do and how much.

Some people get uneasy when they hear about all these practical preparations. Is it because they suspect that these Christians are right? Has God really spoken to them to prepare? Is it possible that it can't be too many years until this second exodus takes place? These are questions that need consideration.

With increasing frequency in the last few years, God has spoken to many people in different countries of Europe and around the world that He will lead His people home to their land from out of the "country of the north" and out of every nation. The many different personal revelations we have heard about, have not been based on imagination, but are rooted in promises in the Bible. We are still awaiting the fulfillment of these promises. We cannot and must not give any dates, but the frequencies of the prophecies and visions on the subject and the many practical preparations of individual Christians are more than remarkable.

Can it be that the time of the final exodus is not far off?

You will have to make your own decision about the answer to that question.

PART III

THE SITUATION OF THE JEWS
IN THE SOVIET UNION

CHAPTER 17

THE HISTORY OF PERSECUTION IN RUSSIA

Why are concerned groups of people around the world demonstrating and speaking out in behalf of the Jews in the Soviet Union, demanding their release? Do actual circumstances inside Russia justify these protests? Is it possible that God has heard the cries of His people and is preparing a way out for them?

Having gained some insight into the prophetic revelations of God in the last section of this book, it will be interesting to take a look behind the Iron Curtain to see if there are signs on the political horizon that would indicate a change of the situation of the Jews in the Soviet Union.

In order to answer these questions, we must begin by taking a look at Jewish history in other countries as well as in the Soviet Union. Unfortunately, we find that the tragedy of Jewish persecution has been a fact throughout the centuries.

Anti-Semitism can be traced back thousands of years to Isaac and Ishmael. God gave the land to Abraham and promised that he would have an heir. But when Sarah passed the child-bearing age, she took matters into her own hands and arranged for the production of an heir for her husband through her Egyptian handmaid, Hagar. When God later miraculously gave Sarah a son, competition arose between her and Hagar. Eventually Hagar and Ishmael were sent away. The two sons and their descendants have been fighting to this day, even though they have a common Semitic heritage.

With the advent of Mohammedism, a further rift developed. The Moslems denounced the Jews for refusing to accept Mohammed as a prophet and therefore the Koran contains some very blatant anti-Semitic traditions.

The strength of the Jewish religion and culture which made it impossible for the Jews to assimilate into other cultures, is the very thing that becomes a threat to totalitarian regimes. Thus we see in history the persecution by people like Pharaoh, Haman, and Herod.

Of all the groups that have persecuted the Jews, the Christians are the most inexcusable, especially since Jesus was a Jew, the first apostles were all Jews, and the writers of the New Testament were Jewish.

In the booklet, *Anti-Semitism, The Persecution of God and His Chosen People*, written by Steffi Rubin and published by Jews for Jesus, the history of Christian persecution is traced. Unfortunately, when

Emperor Constantine made Christianity a state religion in 321 A.D., this not only watered down true Christianity, it brought pressure on the Jews to "convert" or get out. Within three years, legislation was introduced that banned the conversion of anyone to Judaism or the attempt to convert anyone to Judaism. Even before this time, Justin Martyr (d. 167 A.D.) and Origen (d. 251 A.D.) accused Jews of plotting to murder Christians. Eusebius (c. 300 A.D.) alleged that the Jews engaged in the ceremonial killing of Christian children at the holiday of Purim.

The fears generated gave rise to ongoing judgments such as that of John Chrysostom (344-407 A.D.) who said that "there could never be expiation for the Jews," and that "God had always hated them." He called it "incumbent" on all Christians to hate the Jews who he said were "assassins of Christ, and worshippers of the devil." St. Cyril (d. 444 A.D.), Patriarch of Alexandria, gave the Jews within his jurisdiction the choice of conversion, exile, or stoning. St. Jerome (d. 420 A.D.), the celebrated translator of the Latin Vulgate, "proved" in his *Tractate Against Jews* that Jews are "incapable of understanding the Scripture, and that they should be severely prosecuted until they are forced to confess the 'true faith'."

Even St. Augustine (d. 430 A.D.) called Judaism "a corruption" and the Jews "forever guilty and ignorant." He decided that Jews, for their own good, and for the good of the society, "must be relegated to the position of slaves." This theme was later picked up by St. Thomas Acquinas (d. 1274 A.D.) who demanded that the Jews be called to "perpetual servitude." The great reformer, Martin Luther (c. 1544 A.D.), said that the Jews should not merely become slaves, but "slaves of slaves, so that they might not even come into contact with Christians."

During the Crusades in 1099, the Jews in Jerusalem were rounded up into the Great Synagogue. The doors were locked and the synagogue was set on fire. The misguided Crusaders, who had been reared on lies about the Jews, sang "Christ, We Adore Thee" as they marched around the blaze. It has been estimated that 299,000 of the 300,000 Jews in Jerusalem were killed by the Crusaders.

In the Middle Ages the Jews were not entitled to own land and were forced to fill the unsavory post of tax collectors, which only added to their unpopular image. Even the Black Death of 1348, that wiped out a large segment of the European population, was attributed to the poisoning of the wells by Jews. Under severe torture, many Jews "confessed" to the crime.

In the same century, the Archbishop of Canterbury ordered all the Jews exiled from England, forcing them to leave their property to the British government. During the late 1400's, leaders of the Inquisition began persecuting Jews in Spain. Some were tortured or even burned at the stake. In 1492, Ferdinand and Isabella expelled all Jews from Spain. In France and Germany, Christian leaders claimed that "God wills it" as they offered baptism or death to the Jewish residents. Jewish centers grew in Poland, Prussia, and Lithuania, but they suffered severe persecutions during the 1600's.

Steffi Rubin states, "The aged Martin Luther, frustrated by years of non-response to his simple gospel on the part of German Jews, said that the root of their non-response was their evil, devilish nature. In his *Schem Hamphoras*, the Jews were referred to as ritual murderers, poisoners of wells; he called for all Talmuds and synagogues to be destroyed. Many who know little else of Luther have cast him in the same light as the German who rose to power 400 years later and put into action those demands. Those who know of the penitence with which he later reconsidered many of these statements and the work that Luther accomplished toward reform in the church, genuinely regard these expressions of frustration and unkindness with regret and sadness."

It was in Germany in 1879 that the expression "anti-Semitism" was first found in the writings of Wilhelm Marr, *The Victory of Judaism Over Germanism*. In his racist overview, the differences between the Semitic and Aryan groups covered the moral, cultural, linguistic, and physical realms.

Other writers also prepared the way for Hitler to materialize the brewing hatreds and fears that had germinated in the European people. French scientist and rationalist Ernest Renan (1832-1892) made the words "Semitic" and "inferior" to be synonymous. Frenchman Arthur DeGobineau (1816-1882) warned against "cross-breeding" in his *Essay on the Inequality of the Human Races*, an admonition that Hitler would later make law. Houston Stewart Chamberlain (1855-1927) wrote in the *Foundations of the Nine-*

teenth Century in 1899 that the Semitic race was inferior to the Aryan race. Hitler later quoted extensively from this racist book.

All of these things laid the groundwork for the publication of a fraudulent and defamatory work called *Protocols of the Elders of Zion* alleging that it uncovered a plan by which the Jews were seeking to take over the world. Many believed it, even though it had no basis in fact. The *Protocols* had been concocted by the secret police under Czar Nicolas II.

The weak Weimar Republic, set up after the first world war, used the Jews as a scapegoat for all of their problems. Hitler and the Nazi Party took advantage of the situation, exploited the climate for a belief in a master race and the need for a modern day "savior" to rid the country of the troublesome Jews. Racial laws designed to restrict Jewish population were instituted almost immediately with Hitler's takeover in March of 1933. Jews were systematically removed from all public life and leadership. Fifty thousand Jews emigrated from Germany, many to the east.

When the Nuremberg laws cancelled the citizenship of all Jews and intermarriage was forbidden, 200,000 more Jews left Germany. History records the tragic events that followed for the Jews who were not fortunate enough to get out of Germany. Six million Jews, more than twice the number now living in Israel, were heartlessly exterminated. Only four million Jews remained in all of Eastern and Western Europe.

From the time of the middle ages to modern

times, there has been a tremendous increase in the number of Jewish population centers in Eastern Europe. This has been primarily the result of persecutions in Western Europe and Germany.

While in some European countries in the 1700's and 1800's the Jews began to gain rights as free and equal citizens, Jews in Poland and Russia continued to suffer more persecution until the 1900's. Medieval anti-Semitism had been part of life in Russia. Even in the fifteenth century, Ivan the Terrible encouraged it. Later the Jews were blamed for the problems caused by the emancipation of the Russian serfs. By 1880, seventy-five percent of all the Jews in the world lived in Eastern Europe. Until the end of the nineteenth century, there were six million Jews in Russia, which had the greatest migration of Jews of any country in the world.

Because of subsequent persecution and the resultant mass emigration of the Jews toward the West, those numbers were quickly and drastically reduced. After the assassination of Czar Alexander the Second in 1881, a whole wave of pogroms, a Russian word for "an organized massacre or attack," broke loose against the Jews. Businesses were looted, homes devastated, synagogues destroyed, women raped, and many Jewish people killed. Like a fury, it went from one town to another. One hundred and sixty-seven towns and villages in southern Russia were plagued with these acts of terror. While the Czar did not openly condone this persecution, he was glad for the diversion which took pressure off of him. The police did not take steps to protect the Jewish people and so it gave the impression that this attack had been centrally directed.

Panic broke loose among the Jewish population and mass escapes began.

In 1882, the ghettos were instituted and emigration was "encouraged." The regime of Nicolas II (1895-1917) proved to be no better, with the spread of more anti-Semitic propaganda and especially the release of the infamous *Protocols* by Russian newspaper *Znamia* (the Banner) over an eleven-day period at the end of the century. This later-discredited forgery was put forth as the "evidence" for what had always been suspected of the Jewish people. The Jews, tending to be an urban nationality, had been too international for the likes of the strongly nationalistic Russian Empire at the turn of the century. The "League of Russian People," (the Black Hundreds), an organization backed by the government, incited many outbreaks against the Jews, culminating in the Kishinev Massacre in the early 1900's.

An immense stream of refugees had begun to move west toward the borders of Russia. "Before the end of the century (1900), almost one million Jews had left their former homes in Eastern Europe. All of Europe was affected. Every major city in the West, from Stockholm to Lisbon, Paris to London, and Berlin to Vienna were flooded with these poor and hungry refugees. In Germany and Austria, they were rejected. These two countries in the heart of Europe, where the (modern) anti-Semitic propaganda began, remained cold and indifferent. Neither the newspaper articles about the pogroms nor the wretched condition of Jewish refugees brought about any change. Instead of willingness to help, there was unabashed refusal, and voices arose, demanding the blockade of all emigration of Jews from the East. The churches seemed to forget all the commandments in the Bible about helping people in need." [1]

This Jewish persecution in Russia just before the turn of the last century is one of the main reasons for the largest Jewish population in the world today of almost six million in the United States. Many Jews moved on to the United States when European countries refused them. Many of them remained in New York City which now has about two million Jews living within its borders.

Historically, it can be observed that there is a stereotyped pattern of persecution behind any Jewish mass exodus. A growing anti-Semitism at first is only verbally expressed, but ends in forced persecution. Typically, the authorities don't react because the persecution often seems to be a welcome safety valve, letting off the pressure from other social problems.

The Russian Revolution in 1917 turned over the reins of government to Lenin, who decided that since the Jews lacked an important stipulation--a nation--they were not a nationality, but rather a "caste." And it was the goal of communism to dissolve castes. However, at first Lenin did include the Soviet Jews among the minorities to be promised government protection and support in the preservation of their cultural autonomy. In fact, anti-Semitism was outlawed as a punishable counter-revolutionary crime.

So, the situation of the Jews in the Soviet Union improved for awhile. Judaism even became a legal religion. In the constitution, the Jews were recognized as a nationality and in official statistics, ranged twelfth among the different nationalities of the country.

According to R.W. Schloss, "...after the Russian revolution, Jewish cultural institutions, including schools, were supported by the states on a large scale. Yiddish became an officially recognized national language. In the years from 1932 through 1939, the publication of 850 books in Yiddish reached a half a million in print. There were ten theaters with the Yiddish language and about one hundred thousand Jewish children attended schools where Yiddish was taught as a major language."[2]

In 1934 a region in the eastern Siberia part of Russia called "Birobidzhan" was organized as an autonomous Jewish region slated to one day become a Soviet Jewish Republic to counteract the growing Zionist influence. The communists thought this would improve relations with the West. But the Stalinist purges put a brutal end to the project and presently there are only eleven thousand Jews living there among a total of one hundred and eighty thousand Russian citizens. The Kremlin is no longer in favor of a large Jewish population center in a region that has become strategically significant on the Chinese border.

According to Gitta Amipoz in the information briefing pamphlet put out by the Israel Information Center in Jerusalem, *Jews in the Soviet Union,*

"At the peak period of the 1930's, when Jewish creative activity was permitted on the same basis as that of other nationalities, there were about fourteen hundred Yiddish schools, about twenty theatres and theatrical groups, almost twenty daily, weekly, and monthly Yiddish journals, Yiddish publishing houses with an annual output of about two million books and pamphlets, and influential associations of Jewish writers and intellectuals. In areas with large concentrations of Jews, Yiddish existed as an official language in courts and at meetings of local Soviets.

"But the 'Golden Era' was short-lived. Stalin's purges in 1936-38 and then the Nazi invasion of the USSR destroyed much of all that; the anti-Jewish purges in 1948-49 swept away any remnant. Not only was Yiddish culture extinguished, with its chief practitioners put to death, but the very idea of allowing Jews equal cultural expression with other nationalities was unacceptable."

Karl Marx, the father of communism, was himself Jewish, from a line of rabbis. But he did not identify himself as a Jew. His interest in destroying the Jews was an expression of his natural revulsion with religion in general, and with capitalism in particular, a system which he always connected with the Jewish people. Marx believed that, under communism, Jews, and the need for such groups, would disappear.

An atheistic governmental approach is bound to produce anti-Semitism. In spite of the good-sounding promises and laws on paper, there were still major problems. A group of young Jewish militant communists called "the Yevsektsia" attempted to loose the Jewish people from their nationalistic, cultural, and religious loyalties. They enforced the Soviet lifestyle by including work on both religious holidays and the Sabbath, making it impossible to be an observant Jew without also simultaneously appearing to be disloyal to the state.

According to Solomon Schwarz in *The Jews in the Soviet Union*, "the government suppressed synagogue worship, and although fifty or more people could seek a permit for holding religious devotions, there were rules and stigmas imposed upon both the clergy and the worshippers. Religious instruction for children was illegal. The teaching of Hebrew was punishable as well. To be an open 'servant of religion' in any capacity meant one's virtual exclusion from non-religious employment." All this was the case only two years after the revolution.

The attendance in the synagogues declined and simultaneously, the Russians began to undermine the cultural forces of Judaism as well. The deliberate purging of the Jewish scene began in the early thirties. Yiddish newspapers dwindled, Yiddish courts gradually disappeared, and Yiddish theatre, which had been used to disseminate Soviet ideology, declined. All this happened under the proclaimed policy of "non-anti-Semitism."

During this time a new kind of anti-Semitism also

emerged that rose out of the populace rather than the government. Because large numbers of Jewish people had become economically displaced after the revolution, the government came up with the "NEP" (New Economic Policy) and gave these displaced businessmen an opportunity to develop semi-private enterprise. Jew-hatred began to emerge spontaneously. The Jews were accused of all the usual capitalist privilege-grabbing. Finally the advent of the new five-year plans that created more jobs, temporarily halted the wave of anti-Semitism.

In the mid-thirties Joseph Stalin came out as a totalitarian. Although originally against Nazism, Stalin signed a Soviet-Nazi Pact that paved the way for Hitler to exterminate Jews in the Western provinces of the USSR. The toll of Jewish deaths was either left unreported or greatly minimized after the war.

While it has been almost forgotten, it is a fact that right after the founding of the state of Israel in May, 1948, the Soviet Union recognized the new state. After Stalin had strongly supported the founding of the state of Israel, he suddenly turned with hostility against the Jewish state. There are at least three reasons for this. First of all, counter to the expectations of the Soviet Union, Israel had never entertained any thoughts of moving into the communist camp. Instead, she joined the western alliance.

The second reason is that Russia's support for the founding of the state of Israel was not the result of any pro-Israel feelings but rather an anti-British and anti-Colonial stance that backfired.

The third reason may be the internal political considerations caused by the Russian Jews being interested in the new state. As soon as the Soviet Jews proclaimed their sympathy for it, the "Black Years" for Soviet Jews began. Murders and deportations became commonplace during the last five years of Stalin's rule. Accusations of Jewish conspiracy were revived.

Stalin ordered that all Jewish cultural institutions, schools, and printing houses be closed. Jews were arrested just because they practiced Judaism. Those who expressed interest in the state of Israel or Jewish culture received sentences of up to twenty-five years in concentration camps.

The Jew Abraham Schifrin, who had been in concentration camps for ten years from 1953 through 1963 for alleged Zionism, is now living in the free world and gives the following report.

"It was like an atomic explosion as we heard about the state of Israel in 1948. Before 1948, nobody talked about Israel and it did not mean anything to us. But we are Jews and this was sensational for us. Therefore we formed small groups. Nothing special. We tried to find material and shared with each other all the things we knew about Israel.

"As you know, you can find reports about Jewish history in the Bible, in the library, and in encyclopedias. We found some and tried to read and teach each other some things about our early history. Believe me, in 1948 we did not know why this new state had been called Israel. We had not enjoyed any Jewish education. I had been one of the so called "intellectuals," because at one time I had been reading in the Bible and was able to share with my friends something about our early history. But in the eyes of the government, it was a crime and they sent me to prison as a Zionist, even though in the real sense of the word, believe me, I was not a Zionist. But then, in prisons we were really taught.

"Communism in the USSR is completely destroying every Jewish community. There are no Jewish newspapers, magazines, or Jewish clubs to be found in the USSR. All of it is prohibited. Despite the fact that there are two and one-half to three million Jews, the whole country has only...(a few)...synagogues, and spies of the KGB (secret police) are being filtered in constantly. Therefore the Jews know the danger of attending a synagogue.

"The Jewish community is indeed being destroyed. It is impossible to talk in our own language. I can show you letters that will prove it. People went to prison because the KGB found a prayer book and a Hebrew Bible in their house, yes, even a Hebrew language book because they wanted to learn Hebrew. Just that had been their crime and they were sentenced to prison for three, four, or five years. People like Alexandrowitsch and Woloschin and many more were sentenced to concentration camps just for that reason." [3]

Stalin was one of the cruelest Russian leaders. Jewish persecution became rampant. For instance, the Jewish anti-Fascist Committee, composed of prominent Jews and formed during World War II to encourage support for the Soviet war effort among

Jews in the West, was disbanded and most of its members were shot in various campaigns against Jewish "cosmopolitanism" and "Zionism." While the purges stopped and the persecution lessened the year that Stalin died, Russia continued to try to loose Jews from any Jewish loyalty or relations with the outside world. Nikita Khruschev had no love for the Jewish people, and even while denouncing his predecessor's awful crimes against mankind, he conveniently managed to omit those crimes that had been committed against the Jews.

The 1960's saw a continuation of covert anti-Jewish expression, but a new element that was introduced in the Soviet Union was the "Economic Crime." For such cases the penalty was death or a lengthy prison term. It was a guise that enabled persecution to continue without the outward label of anti-Semitism.

In an official publication of the U.S. Government Printing Office, *Fact Sheet on Soviet Jewry* (1972) Richard Maass reports that Judaism, unlike other faiths:

> "Cannot publish periodicals and devotional literature, including journals, prayer books, and Bibles;
> "Cannot produce essential devotional articles such as 'Thalethim' (prayer shawls) or 'Tfilin' (phylacteries);
> "Cannot have regular and official contacts with co-regionalists abroad as contrasted to the experience of Protestant, Catholic, and Moslem

faiths;

"Cannot publish (except in isolated instances, especially in the 'showpiece' Central Synagogue in Moscow) religious calendars, indispensable guides to religious holidays and observances."

In addition to that, there are no Jewish seminaries, and there are no replacements being trained for the few current rabbis. There are no consecrated Jewish cemetaries. Soviet Jews are not allowed to attend international Jewish meetings or to have links with rabbinical or lay Jewish organizations abroad or even to organize on a nationwide basis. These restrictions are for Jews alone and it puts them in virtual isolation.

In 1964, Leonid Brezhnev became head of the Communist Party and Aliksei Kosygin became premier. Although Kosygin parroted the famous statement, "What, me anti-Semite?", the country still treated the Jews with partiality in their ongoing efforts to eliminate any residual identity as a separate nationality. The Soviets had hoped that communist ideology would do away with the Jewish interest in their past culture and religion.

Communism was supposed to satisfy the need for religion and provide a secure base for the people. But the Marxist philosophy of a morality shifting with the economy simply increased the insecurity of the people and an even greater need for religion developed. The Soviet Union wanted to replace the need for God by making the Russian proletariat the object of worship in a class-less, family-less, religion-less society. But when this failed, the communists had to resort to setting apart a particular group, the Jews, to draw fire away from the government. The officially unadmitted anti-Jewish legislation of the 1960's for economic crimes and the overstated anti-Zionism of the 1970's have been said to conceal the fact that socialism has not "improved on capitalism."

And so Brezhnev continued to discriminate against the Jews. During the 1970's, Russian Jews gained worldwide attention when they protested against government attempts to prevent them from emigrating to Israel. World pressure brought some increases in emigration, but under the recent leadership of Yuri Andropov, the attempt to halt Jewish emigration has put up a facade of lies purporting that all Jews who have wanted to leave the Soviet Union have done so. Therefore the Jews in the Soviet Union do remain captive. Alexander Solzhenitsyn, in a newsletter, *Focus on Soviet Jews*, published in November 1971, warned that this type of Soviet annihilation is "...a variation of the gas chambers ...even more cruel because the torture of the people being killed...is more malicious and more prolonged."

In the light of recorded history, it has not been too long ago since that wave of persecution of the Jews in Russia. And, unfortunately, history tends to repeat itself. It is not difficult to imagine that once again millions of Jews from the East could move to the western borders and seek admission into Western Europe, especially since these people are already living under persecution. History indicates that it could be possible at any time. The question is: How will the European nations react this time? How will the government, the public, the churches, and individual Christians react? Will it be similar to their reaction around the turn of the century? Or will they receive the Jewish refugees in spite of the increase of anti-Semitism in the Western world? Will the prophetically prepared Body of Christ be willing to stand with open hearts and reach out with open hands to the Jews, ready to suffer reproach with the children of God and share the impact of the current wave of anti-Semitism?

Increasingly we are finding a rise of anti-Semitism on a world-wide scale. It will not be popular to stand together with the Jewish people.

In the story of Rahab in the second chapter of Joshua, we see that this is nothing new. Here was a woman that understood the ways of God, even though she was not Jewish herself. She harbored two Jewish men, protecting them from those who sought to destroy them. She hid them in her house, and when the authorities were gone, she let them down over the wall, helping them to escape. She endangered her own life to save them.

They told her that she should bring her mother and father and other relatives into her house and that they would all be saved from the destruction that was coming upon the city because of God's judgment. Only Rahab's house and family were spared in the destruction of Jericho. How important it is in any period of time to know God's ways and to cooperate with Him in His plans.

As we stand with the Jewish people, Jesus will stand with us. He explained to the Samaritan woman at the well, *"You worship that which you do not know; we worship that which we know; for salvation is from the Jews"* (John 4:22). They are His special people. He does have special plans for them.

People around the world today are going to be given an opportunity to stand with God's people as He brings them out of Russia and all the other nations, to take them back to the promised land. Those who do will be blessed. Those who take action against God's people or refuse to help them will stand to be judged.

God has given specific and confirmed prophetic revelation about the coming exodus of the Jews out of Russia and has provided time for people to prepare spiritually and practically. It is possible to influence politicians and the public in positive ways, telling them about the coming events that are based on the Word of God as well as the prophetic revelations.

Some may think that the times have changed and that the things of the past like the exodus out of Egypt could not recur. They may point to the pressure of world public opinion and the human rights to which most of the nations adhere. "How can it be possible in our day and age," they ask, "that millions of people would suddenly have to flee from one country to another?"

But here again, recent history shows how easily these things can happen. Who would have thought early in January of 1983 that only a few weeks later two million refugees from Nigeria would pour into the neighboring countries? Neither the world nor the nations next to Nigeria had any advance notice. It came as a sudden blow and presented catastrophic circumstances.

This is the way it happened: "In January of 1983 the governing president Schehu Schagari declared through his Secretary of the Interior that all two million illegal migrant workers were thieves. They alone were accused for the economic breakdown in the country. Without any advanced negotiations with the neighboring nations, he ordered, 'that all foreigners who are illegally in Nigeria will have to leave the country within two weeks'. This launched the greatest expulsion of people in the history of Africa." [4]

The reason for this insane decision was an economic depression. After a tremendous economic upswing through the oil boom, the Nigerian economy plunged into an economic fiasco due to sales recessions and diminishing price levels. During the good years, Nigeria had permitted migrant workers from the destitute regions of the continent to enter by the millions, even illegally, because they were needed. Now they had to leave as scapegoats. How often nations look for someone else to blame when internal problems arise!

It is surely sobering to compare past history with the present. The Russian pogroms around the turn of the century and the recent expulsion of two million migrant workers from Nigeria illustrate that one's imagination does not have to be stretched too far to picture the possibility of a Jewish exodus out of the "country of the north."

CHAPTER 18

PRESENT PERSECUTION

The anti-Semitic actions increased until the death of Stalin and were eagerly continued by his successors. In a secret trial in August of 1952, twenty-six representative Jews were sentenced to death and killed. In January of 1953, fifteen Jewish physicians were accused of plotting to murder the Soviet leaders. Between 1961 and 1963, sixty-eight Jews were executed for alleged economic crimes.

The June 1967 war in Israel raised the level of controversy to new heights. Since that time, the Soviet propaganda has constantly threatened war against Israel and represses and persecutes every Jew who acknowledges Judaism.

In 1977 Abraham Schifrin wrote, "They also tried to agitate in every nation because we have always been the scapegoats in the USSR. It is difficult to describe the living conditions of the Jews in the USSR. Jews do not get good employment and are not allowed to attend educational institutions. Everywhere they are being discriminated against.

"And now the latest from the USSR. You can meet special instigators of the KGB (secret police) on the street, walking like drunks and shouting 'We must kill the Jews because it is their fault that there is starvation in the USSR.' Presently there is a famine, a great famine, but Breshnev is at fault for that and not the Jews. Now they are trying to agitate all the people against the Jews. You know, this is no single case.

"Here I have some letters and I have heard it on telephone conversations too. Friends of mine told me on the telephone just a few days ago, 'You must never forget this and you have to tell everyone, that we are the hostages of murderers.' These Jews are so desperate that they are boldly speaking without fear into the telephone. Try to understand the courage that these people have. Vladimir Margmann was put into a concentration camp for three years because of his telephone conversations with Israel. They are trying to intimidate the people, but they will not be intimidated."[5]

The growing discrimination, the founding of the state of Israel, and the victorious war of June 1967 have strengthened the Jews in Russia and made them more aware of their Jewish background. With the renewal of their Jewish identity, their desire has grown to move back into their own country. This is the reason why more and more Jews are applying for emigration visas for Israel.

The Russian law permits the Jews the right of

emigration for the purpose of reunion with the family. As more and more have wanted to take advantage of their rights, the Soviet leadership has become nervous. At the end of the decade of the sixties, the desire of the Jews to leave the Soviet Union became a mass movement.

For anyone who dares to apply for an exit permit it becomes endless pursuit. "In the beginning of this thorny road to liberty there must be an invitation from relatives in a foreign country. For without that, no application for an emigration visa will be accepted. 'Reunion with the family' will be respected by the authorities of the Soviet Union as a reason for emigration." [6]

If the applicant has this invitation, he must also file a certificate of conduct from the personnel office of his place of employment, with a confirmation of the warden of his city block and a bank statement of his income. The applicant has to pay several fees for the emigration application form, the exit permit, and the renunciation of Soviet citizenship. The average citizen has to work a whole year to save this amount of money. For a large family, this becomes an unusually heavy burden. If the emigration application is rejected, the applicant loses all the fees and has to pay them again with each new application. The applications can be filed only once a year and it is common for the first application to be rejected. Some have to wait as long as five to fifteen years until they get permission. Each year they must again go through the same procedure.

The path of persecution, which can last for years,

begins with the gathering of all these forms for the application. Whenever the applicant requests a certificate or authorization to emigrate, he meets resistance, rejection, mockery, and questioning. Everyone in the city block and at work will be informed and the applicant, and sometimes even his relatives that are not involved become persecuted castaways. Should the permit finally be granted, then the applicant will have to leave the country within a predetermined amount of time, which may be thirty-five days in some provinces, while in others only twelve to twenty days.

During this short period of time, his apartment must be renovated and all formalities taken care of. Often would-be emigrants must reimburse the government for all college education received. Only after all of that is done will it be possible to purchase an airplane or train ticket. In this hectic final phase the applicant can only be at peace when he touches western soil, for some have even been taken back off the airplane or train.

One Jewish man applied for his whole family to leave Russia. The authorities kept him in the country but sent his wife and children out. Over three years later, he's still in Russia. When they first heard that they would be permitted to leave, he took his family to the particular train station where they were told they had to go. It was a long way from the city they lived in.

When they got there, they had to pay a fee under the table to the people who were selling the tickets. And they were charging exorbitant prices because they knew how much people wanted to get out. The graft and corruption was terrible. They just arbitrarily decided how much they were going to charge each person.

Then the family was taken inside the train station and they couldn't leave once they were there. Also the authorities would not let them know when they might be put on the train. They purposely made them wait, without knowing anything.

A train station in Russia is nothing like a station in New York or London. There circumstances are horrible. Once they were in the room, they were informed that they had given up their citizenship. Since they couldn't leave the room they were in, food was brought to them and sold for extremely high prices. The authorities treated them with contempt, making them feel like they were dirt.

After a few days, they sent the wife off on a train without letting the others know her destination. Some days later, they put one of the children on another train to a different destination, and a few days later they put another child on another train in another direction. It was ten days before the third child was sent off on yet another train. They deliberately divided them up and sent them off to different areas to get out of Russia and into Europe. So the children had to travel by themselves without knowing where any of the others would be.

Then, to top it off, the Russian authorities told the father that he could not go at all. He was forced to remain even though they had promised him earlier that he could go. And, of course, they would not tell him where his family had been sent.

Fortunately, the mother and the children knew the city they were to go to, which in this case happened to be Vienna. A special camp had been established there to help Jews coming out of the Soviet Union. It was difficult for the children to find their way, but they and their mother were eventually reunited in Vienna. They did not know at first what had happened to the father.

The father's being kept in Russia even now. He has not seen his family for over three years. And even though the Russians claim that they'll give visas to those who have families outside Russia, they don't honor it.

The father lost his job and now he's a refusenik. They gave him alternative work, a very menial job with about one-third of what it takes to live per month in Russia. It is very difficult for him to afford even the necessities of life. And he does not know if he will ever be reunited with his family.

The persecution can be even more drastic. The home can be searched, possessions can be confiscated, there can be demotion or loss of work, harassment of relatives, the loss of higher education for the children, and even arrest or sentence to heavy labor because of alleged anti-Soviet activities. Even to mention the desire to emigrate is considered criticism of the Soviet Union and is a crime. Sometimes the persecution even becomes sadistic.

There was a family who had a little eleven-year-old girl in the hospital in a particular city in the Soviet Union who was being treated for leukemia. Three

days before the Madrid conference on human rights
was reconvened, the KGB went to the hospital and
took her out. Then they brought the girl to the home
of her parents and just left her there in the living
room. They said, "We don't want you Jewish people
to think that you're going to receive any reprieves or
gain any help because the conference on human rights
is starting up again. We want you to know that things
are going to get tougher for you. And to prove this,
we're going to show you and the whole Jewish community of Russia that your daughter is going to die in
front of your eyes, with absolutely no medical help."
Then they left.

No human mind could have thought up that kind
of thing. It had to come from the pit of hell. But there
was a Jewish agency in the West that found out about
the situation, and they got together the various drugs
that were needed to treat leukemia. They sent this in
by courier with the prescription which was about
twenty-nine written pages long.

These drugs can be lethal, so a person must know
exactly how to use them in ratios of one drug to the
other. There were instructions in the prescription
about what to do if one drug combination didn't work
and certain symptoms happened. It gave all the alter-
natives. It was essential for the parents to have this
twenty-nine-page typewritten prescription to follow
so they could administer the drugs to their little girl.

The police caught the courier at the border and
they took away the prescription but allowed the drugs
to go through. They probably were hoping that the
parents would still administer the drugs without the

prescription, which could easily have killed her, and then the Russians would have had a great propaganda story.

Another courier was sent with the prescription, but he was caught and the prescription taken away. The third courier was also caught, but later the prescription finally did get in.

According to another source, "Some had to battle for years to leave the country, others received the permit without any problem, and again others are still sitting in camps today because they are considered to be activists or mouthpieces of the movement. In the fall of 1977, there were at least twenty-one Jewish activists in camps or in internal exile. From 1978 until October 1980, twelve additional leaders of the Jewish emigration movement were sentenced to camps of internal exile or were put into psychiatric wards. This same double strategy is also being used in the Soviet Union against massive or spontaneous opposition movements from the underground. Even sympathizers are not given any relief by the police, judicial courts, and Soviet leadership. In this way the Soviets are trying to stamp out any such growing movement." [7]

The wave of those who wanted to emigrate could not be broken by the massive governmental resistance and reprisal. Even the continual harassment of the Jews was not able to stop their determination to apply for emigration.

During the decade of the seventies, most emigration applicants were relatively successful. "Since the beginning of this exodus in 1971 until 1980, about two

hundred and fifty thousand Jews have left the USSR,
even though the annual emigration quota fluctuated
tremendously. The permits reached thirty-five thousand in 1973 and peaked with fifty-one thousand in
1979. The expansion of the quota had a direct relationship to the Soviets' desire to influence American
politicians during the SALT I and II negotiations or
to increase commerce." [8]

After 1979, there seemed to be a change in
politics concerning exit permits. The numbers began
to decrease at an alarming rate and now in 1983 only
about a hundred Jews a month are allowed to
emigrate. Something seems to be in the air. The major German newspaper *Frankfurt Allgemeine Zeitung
(Frankfurt General News)* issued March 16, 1983
reports, "Since 1979, the number of Soviet Jews to be
permitted to leave the Soviet Union, according to the
world conference, has been drastically reduced. While
in 1979, 51,320 Jews emigrated, there were only
21,471, 9,447, and 2,668 in the following years. In the
first month of 1982 only 204 Jews were permitted to
leave the Soviet Union." (See graph.)

The same article continues, "The conference
board also reported further that 400,000 Jews are
planning to emigrate from the Soviet Union. About
7,000 have received official notification that their
emigration would not be permitted. Many of these
Jews have been waiting from five to twelve years to
emigrate. Tens of thousands of those Jews who have
applied have never received any answer on their application from the government agencies. The conference board mentioned further that all activists

LATEST NEWS FROM THE USSR

JEWISH EMIGRATION FROM THE USSR

Soviet Jewry emigration figures from 1979 to 1982 show a dramatic decline. In the first quarter of 1983, only 404 Jews left the USSR. Experts estimate that less than 2000 Soviet Jews will be able to make aliyah this year.

Year	Emigration
1970	4,235
1971	13,022
1972	31,681
1973	34,733
1974	20,628
1975	13,221
1976	14,261
1977	16,736
1978	28,864
1979	51,320
1980	21,471
1981	9,447
1982	2,688

Scale: 5,000 — 10,000 — 15,000 — 20,000 — 25,000 — 30,000 — 35,000 — 40,000 — 45,000 — 50,000 — 55,000 — 60,000

This graph appeared in the May 1983 issue of the Quarterly Report of the Union of Councils for Soviet Jews, 1411 K Street N.W., Washington, D.C. 20005.

among the Soviet Jews are being systematically persecuted and intimidated. Their homes are being searched, Jewish books confiscated, Hebrew language courses are prohibited, as well as scientific seminars.

"American Jewish leaders, who had just returned to Israel from a visit in the Soviet Union, talked about 'a turn for the worse' for the Soviet Jews. A growing anti-Semitism has also led to assaults against the Jews who have never even applied for an exit visa. The Americans further reported that a game is being played in schools which is called 'concentration camps.' One child, who is generally Jewish, gets a number and for several days the classmates call this child just by the number instead of the child's name."

The above recent reports would indicate that the situation of the Jews in the Soviet Union has really become critical. Because of this, various organizations are trying to focus world attention on this dramatic problem.

In 1980 for the first time, the World Jewish Congress (WJC) with other organizations from France, Italy, and the Netherlands, "together took the initiative to point out the needs of the Jewish minority in the Soviet Union, within the framework of the Madrid followup conference to the Conference of Security and Cooperation in Europe (KSZE) that was held in Helsinki where they pleaded for decisive results." [9]

The Jewish weekly paper in Germany, *Allgemeine Judische Wochenzeitung (General Jewish Weekly)*, reports in their issue of March 4, 1983 that "the European Community representatives have been advised that the Soviet Union is squeezing the numbers of Jewish emigrants year by year and in January of 1983 only eighty-one Jews have been allowed to leave. The ambassador to the European Common Community (ECC) received our request very seriously, especially our concern for the maintenance of the Jewish identity in the Soviet Union which for them is a general problem of human rights."

One thousand delegates from thirty-one countries met on March 15, 1983, at the third Jewish World Conference for Soviet Jewry. Prominent personalities who had just visited the Soviet Union reported about the discriminating actions of the Soviet regime against the Jews.

"According to the conference board, there are two and one-half million Jews living in the Soviet Union who are systematically being separated from their historical and religious roots. Professionally, the Jews are being disadvantaged and barred from the university. For over one generation, there have been no new rabbis. No religious leaders in the Soviet Union have been able to receive training. Hundreds of synagogues have been closed. The Hebrew language is prohibited and there are no newspapers, books, radio, or TV programs referring to Jewish culture. According to this report, Jews who are applying for emigration will be punished immediately by losing their place of work and academic rank as well as membership in scientific circles." [10]

About the same time in the spring of 1983, the "European Woman's Conference on Soviet Jewry" was held in Geneva, Switzerland, discussing the same subject. The proclamations and demonstrations in front of the Russian embassies in many different cities continue to express the concern of people in the free world for the plight of the Russian Jews.

In May 1983, concerned Jewish and Christian groups helped to sponsor a full-page advertisement prepared by the Center for Russian Jewry head-quartered in New York. The title reads, IN AMERICA, YOU HAVE TO KILL SOMEONE TO GET 12 YEARS IN PRISON. -- IN RUSSIA, YOU MAY JUST HAVE TO TEACH HEBREW.

The text states that,

"On November 6, 1982, Dr. Joseph Begun of Moscow was arrested. Now, after 6 months of KGB interrogation, he faces trial and sentence. For the third time. For up to 12 years. In a forced labor camp.

"Not for murder or manslaughter. Not for armed robbery or arson. But for privately teaching, in a country where more than 100 languages are spoken and dozens more are taught and studied, the one that is forbidden: Hebrew.

"All across the Soviet Union, Jews who try to transmit their heritage face arrest, trial, and imprisonment as serious 'threats' to Soviet law and order.

"Yuri Tarnopolsky, for example, who taught in a Jewish Free University in Kharkov, is ex-pected to be tried in May. Dr. Alexander Parit-sky, its founder, is already undergoing savage treatment in a slave labor camp. So is Felix Kochubiyevsky of Novosibirsk, who tried to set up a Soviet-Israel Friendship Society. Simon Shnirman of Kerch has again been sentenced for wanting to join his elderly father in Israel.

"Yaakov Mesh of Odessa is in danger of arrest for Jewish educational activities. Lev Elbert of Kiev has just been charged. Even a respected scholar like Ilya Essas of Moscow, known for his scrupulous compliance with Soviet law, cannot conduct a small private study group without constant fear of KGB interference."

The text ends with the challenge that surely

"American people will not sit idly by while 3 million human beings are condemned to a spiritual gas chamber. Because that would be the biggest crime of all."

Even the President of the United States is putting pressure on Russia to permit Jewish emigration. In an article that appeared in the February 3rd issue of the *Toronto Globe and Mail* titled "Reagan Urges Soviets to Let Jews Emigrate," Reagan said, "Jews face adversity in the Soviet Union, are denied basic rights to study and practice their religion, and are subjected to brutal harassment if they want to emigrate. We will not forget them. Make no mistake. We seek better relations with the Soviet Union, but we've made it plain now we want deeds, not rhetoric and repression from the new Soviet leadership. We've had enough of words. There is no better way for them to begin than by releasing the prisoners of conscience in Siberia and restoring Jewish emigration to the levels of the late 1970's."

A few weeks after the third World Convention of
Soviet Jewry in Jerusalem, an article entitled "An
Appeal" was published in *Pravda* on April 3, 1983,
urging people throughout the Soviet Union to help ex-
pose and stamp out Zionism. It was the first official
action of the newly-formed Anti-Zionist Committee
established by the Soviet government.

The May, 1983, issue of the *Union of Councils for
Soviet Jews Quarterly Report* stated:

"The formation of an 'anti-Zionist Committee of
the Soviet Public' was announced on March 31, 1983,
in one of the most frightening aspects yet of the
Kremlin's anti-Semitic campaign. Under this
manifesto, any Soviet Jew who openly strives to
emigrate may be classified as an enemy of the state
and treated accordingly.

"The Committee's declaration was signed by
eight Jews. Two of the signatories, General David
Dragunsky and law professor Samuel Sivs, made
public statements in the past denouncing Russian
Jews who seek to emigrate, and Israel. The other
signers included writers Genrikh Grofman and Yuri
Kolesnidov, Lenin Prize winner Martin Kabachnik,
history professor Gregory Bondarevsky, filmmaker
Boris Shenin, and philosopher Henrikas Zimanos.

"The manifesto lashed out against Zionism as 'a
concentration of extreme nationalism, chauvinism,
racial intolerance, justification of territorial seizure
and annexation, armed adventurism, a cult of political
arbitrariness and impunity, demagogy and idealogical
sabotage, sordid maneuvers and perfidy.' It de-

nounced 'the reckless adventurist policies of the Israeli Zionists as a source of trouble and suffering not only for the Arab people,' and claimed that 'in its global strategy, imperialism widely uses international Zionism as a strike force for an offensive against socialism. Usurping the right to "defend" Soviet Jews, the Zionist ringleaders try to persuade world opinion that a "Jewish question" allegedly exists in the USSR.' Soviet Jews angrily denounce such slander.

"The declaration urged intellectuals, workers, and farmers to be active in the 'political exposure of Zionism and firmly rebuff its intrigues.' Journalists, writers, artists, and scholars were called upon to "more fully reveal in your works and statements the anti-people and anti-humanitarianism of the diversionary propaganda policy of Zionism.' The appeal suggests that the Kremlin is planning a broad campaign to this end."

Even though eight prominent Jews allowed their names to be placed at the end of this appeal, it was obvious that they had done so only because of Soviet pressure on them, possibly having their positions threatened.

One of the men who signed the article, a Jewish general named Dragunsky, appeared on prime-time television to explain why Zionism was a force that must be stopped. He challenged everyone to be on the alert for any Zionist activities and to report these to the authorities immediately.

The State Department of the United States sharply criticized the Committee's attack against

Zionism, calling it an "anti-Semitic diatribe".

On June 6, 1983, the Soviet Anti-Zionist Committee held a press conference in Moscow. As would be expected, they made some unfounded assertions:

1) that the reunification of divided families has "been essentially completed;"

2) that the "vast majority of Jews who wish to leave the Soviet Union have already received permission to depart;"

3) that anti-Semitic discrimination does not exist in the Soviet Union — and that Zionism is a "man-hating ideology" which is "increasingly modeled on the ideas and methods of Hitler."

The Union of Councils for Soviet Jews published an open letter of rebuttal in the *New York Times* on June 12, 1983 saying:

1) that family reunification is not completed, that there are thousands of people in the U.S. and Israel who "yearn to be reunited with their loved ones barred from leaving the Soviet Union."

2) that "hundreds of thousands would leave if given the opportunity. In fact, more than 750,000 have begun to apply for exit visas by asking for invitations from Israel, and only 260,000 of these people have emigrated."

3) that "anti-Semitism is the cornerstone of your government's policy. It is in your newspapers, television programs, the magazines you produce for your children, the training you give to your soldiers, and in the admissions policies of your universities." They went on to charge that anti-Semitism is even manifested in the slanderous Russian description of

Zionism as "something akin to Hitlerism."

An article from the June 9 edition of the *Washington Times* reported Representative Benjamin Gilman as saying, "The Soviet Union has created a 'Catch-22' to prevent thousands of Jews from emigrating--making letters of invitation from abroad mandatory, then intercepting the mail." He went on to report that "a year-long investigation by the Post Office and Civil Service Committee"--of which he is a member--"has produced over 200 pieces of evidence that the Soviet authorities are tampering with the mail of its citizens."

Surely we can recognize all of this as a reaction to the increasing pressure from the people in the Western world. Instead of lessening their persecution of the Jews, the Soviets are increasing their policy of anti-Semitism. People who have visited the Soviet Union in the spring of 1983, document that Russia is becoming even more like a "big concentration camp" for the two and one-half to three million Jews living there.

We personally visited one man who for eleven years was denied the right to leave. He was a World War II airplane pilot, one of the most decorated heroes of the Soviet Union. He and his wife and his daughter applied to emigrate to Israel. They allowed his daughter to go but they would not allow him or his wife to leave. They've been separated for many years. His wife had had a serious heart disease for years and she died just a few months ago from a heart attack.

They've gone through so much harassment for years and years that he finally sent all his medals back to the Soviet government in protest of his situation. He had the highest medal that a Russian could receive as a citizen. He even sent that back and said that he wanted to leave.

But they told him he couldn't leave because he had military secrets. He's been retired out of the armed forces of the Soviet Union for over twenty years. What could he know that isn't obsolete?

Persecution in the Soviet Union is by no means restricted to the Jews. It also includes other religious groups, especially fundamentalist Christians. The March 1983 issue of *The Voice of Martyrs* reported, "In twelve years, the Soviet Communists arrested 25,000 Baptist pastors; 22,000 died in concentration camps and 1,000 Christians are known to be in jail now in the USSR alone. Who knows how many have disappeared into the Gulag?"

The well publicized "Siberian Seven," who raced past Soviet guards into the American Embassy five years ago to seek freedom to practice their Christian faith without persecution, have brought the plight of Russian Christians into public notice. It is estimated that the two families, the Vashchenkos and the Chmykhalovs, are only representative of about 30,000 Russian Pentecostals who are seeking to emigrate. They are seldom allowed to do so.

The Vashchenko family, who has had a history of twenty-three years of continual emigration refusal, was granted permission to emigrate to Israel on June 27, 1983. News media pressure was cited as the probable reason for their exit.

The United Press release that appeared in major

newspapers across the United States said that "it was
not thought likely that the breakthrough in the
Vashchenko case signaled a lasting change in Soviet
reluctancy to allow citizens to leave the country."

The July 17, 1983 issue of *The Seattle Times*
reported that "the last two of the seven
Pentecostalists who lived at the U.S. Embassy in
Moscow...have been given permission to emigrate
from the Soviet Union, the State Department said
yesterday. Maria Chmykhalov and her son, Timofei,
were enroute yesterday from their home in Siberia to
Moscow, along with twelve other family members.
They were expected to arrive tomorrow in Vienna,
said the Rev. Blahoslav Hruby, editor of a documen-
tary journal, *Religion in Communist Dominated
Areas*. He said that the family was expected to settle
in the United States."

The official Russian news agency Tass had the
audacity to quote Samuel Zivs, a Jewish lawyer who is
a member of the recently formed anti-Zionist committee in Russia, as saying that "he thought most Soviet
Jews who wanted to join relatives abroad had done so
and that there was no need for more to leave."

Western analysts estimate "there are some
20,000 to 30,000 Soviet Jews who have been refused
permission to emigrate and many thousands more
who are still waiting word on exit visa applications."
Most total estimates approach 400,000 to 500,000.

While there are quite a few organizations that
publicize the plight of the Russian Christians, there
are only a handful of groups doing the same for the
Russian Jews. It is important that people all over the

world pray for and work for the release of all persecuted people who desire to leave the Soviet Union, Jew and Christian alike.

CHAPTER 19

THE EMERGING PHARAOH

The various reports about the present situation of the Jews in the Soviet Union and the attention of world public opinion does not surprise those who have heard from God prophetically about the exodus of the Jews "out of the country of the north." The reports simply confirm the truth. Today's events in the Soviet Union show an interesting parallel to the situation of the children of God in Egypt. The Bible points out that the final exodus out of the "land of the north" can be compared with the exodus from Egypt.

In Jeremiah 16:14,15 we read, *" 'Therefore behold, days are coming,' declares the Lord, 'when it will no longer be said, "As the Lord lives, who brought up the sons of Israel out of the land of Egypt," but "As the Lord lives, who brought up the sons of Israel from the land of the north and from all the countries where He had banished them." For I will restore them to their own land which I gave to their fathers.' "*

All the recent prophecies and visions that we know about confirm that this is about to happen.

Remember the situation in Egypt. At first the circumstances turned worse and worse. The new Pharaoh was far more cruel than his predecessor and the pressure against the Hebrew people intensified. Then through the ministry of Moses, God sent plagues to Egypt which ultimately led to the release of the Hebrew nation and the ensuing exodus.

Since November of 1982, the Soviet Union has also had a new "Pharaoh" by the name of Yuri Andropov. Remember the report of the prayer meeting in Sweden in March of 1982 where the Spirit of God revealed that there would be a change in leadership in the Kremlin. Looking at the career of Yuri Andropov, it is not difficult to draw the parallel to the type of "Pharaoh" of those former days.

In the December 1982 issue of the *Dokument and Analyse* we read, "To differentiate Andropov from his predecessors, it is for the first time that a chief of the KGB (secret police) has moved to the head of the party. He embodies a new type of Soviet leadership."

The commentary of another newspaper reads, "It shows a new respectability to this government agency (KGB), that their chief now has become the party boss. An agency with great similarity to the Gestapo, in that it has twenty-five thousand employed policemen and agents, with the border troops under its command and approximately ten thousand part-time agents at hand." [11]

Yet another newspaper reports, "During his fifteen years with the KGB, the raising up and complete liquidation of the dissident movements have occurred. He is responsible for the expulsion of Solschenizyn, the banishment of Sacharow, and the induction of completely healthy Soviet citizens into psychiatric prison wards because they fought for human rights. During his time in office, the so-called Helsinki* groups were annihilated, and many religious and anti-Russian opponents were arrested." [12]

This would be enough of the commentaries to draw a picture of the new chief in the Kremlin. But there's more. Beginning with his time in office, permissions for emigration of the Jews were almost completely stopped. A new wind is blowing in the Kremlin. Heinz Abosch writes, "Anti-Jewish accents in Soviet policies are always symptoms of a hardening of attitude. The policies tend to occur in periods of increasing dictatorial rule because of internal and external political tensions and tend to decrease in times of liberalization." [13] As an outsider of the Kremlin, it will be difficult for Andropov to maintain his authority. He will be envied and accused by others. It will be easy for him to dredge up the old proven "scapegoat" theory to distract from the real problems.

For years agricultural failure has been the greatest internal problem area in the Soviet Union. For four years Russian farming has been plagued by

---

*   The Helsinki agreement signed in August 1975 by Brezhnev guaranteed certain freedoms to the Russian people. These Helsinki groups were started to monitor the Russian compliance with these agreements.

extreme weather conditions and the food supply for the population has reached a critically low level. Could this be one of God's judgments to get His people released? It is interesting to notice a quotation from a newspaper which carried Andropov's 'State of the Nation' address which had been released by the Soviet news agency, Tass. Speaking to the province party-chiefs and drawing this parallel to the subject of farming it stated, "It is characteristic that he (Andropov) gave no agricultural statistics. The situation has not changed. The party-boss felt reminded of biblical 'plagues.' In recent years the weather has had a catastrophical influence on the harvest. Grain harvest figures are not even being released." [14]

It is further interesting to note that the destructive weather patterns that have caused such extensive crop failures began when the Soviets choked off the flow of Jewish emigration.

As this book was in the final stage of being written, the United Press report from Moscow on June 16, 1983 carried the headline: "Andropov consolidates power as head of Soviet Union." The article read:

"Communist Party chief Yuri Andropov today was named President of the Soviet Union, consolidating his control over the Kremlin by accumulating, in seven months, the power it took Leonid Brezhnev thirteen years to assume.

"Andropov's election by the Soviet legislature gives him the three top titles held by Brezhnev on his death in November — president, Communist Party chief, and chairman of the defense council.

" 'Your trust in me I consider trust placed in the Communist Party of the Soviet Union, and I have been a member of this party for more than forty years, and I adhere to its ideals,' Andropov said after the unanimous vote was taken by a show of hands."

Andropov admits that he is the epitome of the Communist ideals. Unfortunately, these ideals include the ongoing persecution of the Jewish people in a country that has more than 100 nationalities.

The press release went on to say that "Politburo member Konstantin Chernenko, who was out-maneuvered by Andropov to succeed Brezhnev, put Andropov's name up for nomination and said Andropov 'will meet the highest and best interests of the state.'

"Chernenko praised Andropov's 'energetic and imaginative activity that has brought him the 'general respect, faith, and sympathy of the party and people'.

"Andropov showed no emotion after the vote ...when he rose to acknowledge the standing ovation from members of the Supreme Soviet, the nation's legislature, meeting in joint session."

The article continued to explain that "Brezhnev became Communist Party leader in 1964, but he did not add the presidency and chairmanship of the defense council to his political responsibilities until 1979. (Andropov's appointment as defense chief was announced in May.)

"The presidency, known formally as the chairmanship of the presidium of the Supreme Soviet, is largely a figurehead post with mainly ceremonial duties, but it puts Andropov on the same protocol footing as powerful chiefs of state such as Reagan and French President Francois Mitterrand."

In January of 1983, fifty leading experts on Soviet affairs from North America, Europe, and Israel met at the London School of Economics and Political Science. They gave a gloomy analysis of the prospects for Soviet Jewry emigration. One report said, "The experts, including Prof. Richard Pipes, a former member of the U.S. National Security Council, agreed that there had been a serious deterioration in the status of Soviet Jews and that Yuri Andropov's initial statements seemed to foreshadow further repression of minority national cultures in the USSR."

The scene has now been set. The man, who has been the "strongman" head of the Secret Police (KGB) has now become President of the Soviet Union. Will the new Pharaoh be more cruel than his predecessor? What will be the new pressures on the Russian Jews? And, when will God send "a ministry of Moses" to confront Andropov and boldly proclaim with God's anointing that he must "let My people go!?"

PART IV

THE BIBLICAL EVIDENCE
FOR THE FINAL EXODUS

CHAPTER 20

THE BIBLE VERIFIES THE PROPHECIES

All prophetic revelations must be examined on the basis of the Word of God. The experiences, prophecies, and visions may be inspiring and sound convincing, but if they are not rooted in the Bible, we cannot count on their being true. However, if the Bible verifies the testimonies of all the people mentioned in this book who have had a fresh revelation that God is in indeed going to bring His people out of the "country of the north," then we have a truth that needs to be proclaimed throughout the world.

Just what does the Bible have to say concerning the children of God returning to their promised land? The Bible surely presents us with much evidence that we are living "in the last days." The events concerning Israel have always been God's indicator on the clock of world history. God's promise that the Jews will return to their land is like a thread that runs throughout the Bible. Hope for the realization of this

promise began with the establishment of the state of
Israel in 1948. Bible-believing Christians are waiting
for this great event of the exodus of the Jews out of
the land of the north and out of every nation of the
world into Israel as the preparation for the return of
Jesus, the Messiah.

Why is it that we can say with such great confidence that we are living "in the last days?" It is
simply because many of the prophecies about the
children of God are being fulfilled in front of our eyes.
The prophet Hosea says, *"For the sons of Israel will
remain for many days without king or prince, without
sacrifice or sacred pillar, and without ephod or
household idols. Afterward the sons of Israel will
return and seek the Lord their God and David their
king; and they will come trembling to the Lord and to
His goodness in the last days"* (Hosea 3:4,5).

We are experiencing in our time the fulfillment of
that scripture. For centuries the children of Israel
have been without a king. The King of kings came to
them, but they did not accept Him. They are without a
prince because they have rejected the "Prince of
peace."

In the year 70 A.D., Titus conquered Jerusalem
and destroyed the temple. Since that time, the Jews
have not been able to make sacrifices because there
has been no place for them to sacrifice unto God. This
is what Hosea had proclaimed a long time before the
destruction of the temple. For almost two thousand
years the Jews have been without "sacrifice" and
without the "robe of the priest." They have been
dispersed into the four corners of the earth. The

world is an eyewitness to that.

But pay special attention to verse five, *"After-ward the sons of Israel will return and seek the Lord their God and David their King; and they will come trembling to the Lord and to His goodness in the last days."* It is the plan of God that the Jews, by their return, will seek the Lord their God and David their king. Of whom is Hosea talking? The name of David is mentioned, but the interesting part is that David was already dead when Hosea spoke these words. Therefore, he is speaking of the One who would come out of the house of David, the Messiah.

This prophetic verse tells us something about the time of the return of the Messiah. *"...they will come trembling to the Lord and to His goodness in the last days."* According to the Bible, this occurrence will take place at a specific time in God's redemptive plan, "in the last days"–which means at the end of the time of world history as we know it. The prophetic word says that in the last days the Jews will first return to Israel and then they will find their God and Messiah.

On May 14, 1948, Israel became a sovereign state. Since that time, it has been possible for Jews to return to the land that God promised the heirs of Abraham, Isaac, and Jacob. Just this event alone shows us that humanity will soon see the return of the Messiah. This time He will come as a King. Jesus will return soon! But before He returns, certain things will have to come to pass to prepare the way for Him.

Here we can see a people returning to their own land after two thousand years. It is still one nation, despite dispersion and persecution. They are still speaking the language of their forefathers. They are still celebrating the feasts as they did centuries ago. They still pray to the God of their forefathers. It is a great miracle, yet many people in the world do not recognize it. But in all of world history, never has such a thing happened to any other nation. After two thousand years, the Jews are returning to their own land because the Bible is true and God keeps His Word.

Many of us have witnessed these events in our own lifetime. God has kept His Word concerning His people. It makes our hearts rejoice! If God did not keep His Word of the Old Covenant with His Jewish people, how would we know that He will keep His Word concerning future events? It's because we see that He has kept His promises with His people that we have the hope and faith and confidence in our hearts that He will indeed keep all of His promises that are to be fulfilled in the future.

God's promises concerning Israel have always been fulfilled. In Isaiah 35:1 we read, *"The wilderness and the desert will be glad, and Arabah (the desert) will rejoice and blossom; like a crocus."* Anyone who has been to Israel will confirm that the desert is being watered and blossoming like a flower garden. By this, we can see that the Word of God is true even in the smallest details. Here is another promise coming to pass after more than two thousand years. It is a miracle; ongoing evidence that God's Word is true!

We read in Isaiah 27:6, *"In the days to come Jacob will take root, Israel will blossom and sprout; and they will fill the whole world with fruit."* Wherever I have gone in Europe, I have had the opportunity to eat "Jaffa oranges". The Bible promised us that "the fruit of Israel will fill the whole earth." It is happening today.

1 Kings 8:56 tells us that all of God's promises will be fulfilled, *"Blessed be the Lord, who has given rest to His people Israel, according to all that He promised; not one word has failed of all His good promise, which He promised through Moses His servant."* It is important for us to understand the Word of God so that we may comprehend the ways of God. In the Bible we can read how God deals with His people and that all His promises concerning His people will find their fulfillment. Just as everything has come to pass that God had promised to Moses concerning the exodus out of Egypt, so we will be able to expect the promise of the exodus out of the north to happen.

After the Lord had led His people into the promised land, the children of Israel realized, *"Not one of the good promises, which the Lord had made to the house of Israel failed; all came to pass"* (Joshua 21:45). Some of the last words that Joshua spoke to the nation just before his death were, *"You know with all your heart and soul that not one of all the good promises the Lord your God gave you has failed. Every promise has been fulfilled; not one has failed"* (Joshua 23:14 NIV).

God will fulfill every promise concerning His people Israel, whether pertaining to former days or to the future.

*Then the word of the Lord came to me say-
ing, "Son of man, what is this proverb you
people have concerning the land of Israel,
saying, 'The days are long and every vision
fails'? Therefore say to them, 'Thus says the
Lord God, "I will make this proverb cease so
that they will no longer use it as a proverb in
Israel." But tell them, "The day draws near
as well as the fulfillment of every vision. For
there will no longer be any false vision or flat-
tering divination within the house of Israel.
For I the Lord shall speak, and whatever
word I speak will be performed. It will no
longer be delayed, for in your days, O
rebellious house, I shall speak the word and
perform it," declares the Lord God.' Furthermore, the word of the Lord came to me
saying, "Son of man, behold, the house of
Israel is saying, 'The vision that he sees is for
many years from now, and he prophesies of
times far off.' Therefore say to them, 'Thus
says the Lord God, "None of My words will
be delayed any longer. Whatever word I
speak will be performed," ' " declares the
Lord God* (Ezekiel 12:21-28).

Today we can see how many promises have
already been completed. Israel is a nation. Hebrew
again is a living language. The desert is blooming.
The fruits of Israel are filling the whole earth. One
prophecy after another is coming to pass in our time.

In Jeremiah 31:35-37 we are told, *"Thus says the*

Lord, who gives sun for light by day, and the fixed order of the moon and the stars for light by night, Who stirs up the sea so that its waves roar; the Lord of hosts is His name: 'If this fixed order departs from before Me,' declares the Lord, 'then the offspring of Israel shall also cease from being a nation before Me forever.' Thus says the Lord, 'If the heavens above can be measured, and the foundations of the earth searched out below, then I will also cast off the offspring of Israel for all that they have done,' declares the Lord."

Even though some would like to see things differently, God has not cast off His people and He will fulfill His Word concerning them. Not because they have deserved it, but because God says so in His Word. We need to understand God's ways. If man can bypass God's order of nature and search out the foundations of the heavens and the earth, then He will cast away the offspring of Israel. To do that would be impossible! Man will not be able to search out God's order and push it aside. Therefore, God will stay with His people, *"For I, the Lord, do not change; therefore you, O sons of Jacob, are not consumed"* (Malachi 3:6).

No matter how consistently Satan is trying to kill every single Jew, the sons of Jacob will not be consumed, for God does not change His decisions. He is faithful in His promises. No matter how the battle rages to shake Israel, this nation will stand till Jesus returns: *"Then the Lord your God will restore you from captivity, and have compassion on you, and will gather you again from all the peoples where the Lord your God has scattered you. If your outcasts are at the ends of the earth, from there the Lord your God will*

*gather you, and from there He will bring you back.
And the Lord your God will bring you into the land
which your fathers possessed, and you shall possess it;
and He will prosper you and multiply you more than
your fathers. Moreover the Lord your God will circumcise your heart and the heart of your descendants,
to love the Lord your God with all your heart and with
all your soul, in order that you may live"*
(Deuteronomy 30:3-6).

This is the Word of God for His people, regardless
of where they have been scattered. No matter what
the distance happens to be, God will gather them out
of every nation and bring them back into the land that
He had promised to their fathers. We will witness
these things as they happen. God keeps His covenant
with his Jewish people. He will bring them back into
the land of their fathers and will circumcise their
hearts so that they will be spiritually renewed. God's
Word is true! This is His plan for "the last days" as
presented in the third chapter of Hosea. With the
establishment of the state of Israel in 1948, the beginning of the end of human history as we know it has
been marked.

CHAPTER 21

THE SECOND EXODUS WILL ECLIPSE
THE FIRST ONE

Jeremiah 30:3 states, " *'For, behold, days are coming,' declares the Lord, 'When I will restore the fortunes of My people Israel and Judah.' The Lord says, 'I will also bring them back to the land that I gave to their forefathers, and they shall possess it.'* "

Zephaniah 3:20 continues, " *'At that time I will bring you in, even at the time when I gather you together; indeed, I will give you renown and praise among all the peoples of the earth, when I restore your fortunes before your eyes,' says the Lord.*"

These are His unchangeable promises. God will gather the Jews and lead them back into the land of their forefathers. And not only that, He will give Israel honor among all the nations of the earth as God removes their captivity before the eyes of all mankind.

While it is true that the Jews have been scattered everywhere in the world, it is also true that they shall return out of every nation to the nation of Israel. The return, which we may call "the second exodus," will affect all the nations of the world. It will begin in the "land of the north" and it will spread to all the nations of the earth. The exodus of the Russian Jews will trigger the return of Jews from all over the world to Israel.

Bible verses that speak of the significant part in God's plan for the second exodus include Isaiah 11:11,12: *"Then it will happen on that day that the Lord will again recover the second time with His hand the remnant of His people, who will remain, from Assyria, Egypt, Pathros, Cush, Elam, Shinar, Hamath, and from the islands of the sea. And He will lift up a standard for the nations, and will assemble the banished ones of Israel, and will gather the dispersed of Judah from the four corners of the earth."*

The thought that catches our attention immediately is that the Lord *"will again recover the second time with His hand."* The question arises, "When was the first time?" Exodus, the second book of Moses, describes the first "coming out" of Egypt of the children of God. Some may think that the return of the Jews out of the Babylonian captivity was the second exodus. That cannot be, for the return from Babylon was not a worldwide homecoming; it was restricted to the region of Babylon. The text calls for a homecoming from "the four corners of the earth and the islands of the sea." This means that this last exodus will be from the four directions around the earth which would include all the continents of this world. That kind of homecoming has not yet taken place.

We are also told in these verses that God will do something so outstanding that it will be a sign to the nations of the world, *"And He will lift up a standard for the nations..."* What sign could be more outstanding than another exodus of the Jews, but this time being from all the nations around the earth? God loves the nations of the world and He longs for them to come to know Him and serve Him. Therefore He will demonstrate before the nations of the world that He is the God of Israel. The standard He will raise up will be this mighty worldwide exodus of His people, something only the true and living God could orchestrate. The impact will be that the nations will be amazed and many will turn from their self-centered, humanistic, sinful way of life and prepare themselves for the return of the Messiah.

In Isaiah 43:16-19 we find the verses related to the move of the Hebrew nation through the Red Sea. *"Thus says the Lord, who makes a way through the sea and a path through the mighty waters, Who brings forth the chariots and the horse, the army and the mighty man. (They will lie down together and not rise again; they have been quenched and extinguished like a wick)."* Isaiah describes how God opened the Red Sea and enabled the children of Israel to move through it. But verse 17 tells us that the waters of the Red Sea covered the army of Pharaoh and destroyed it. Verse 18 goes on, *"Do not call to mind the former things or ponder things of the past!"* Here Isaiah tells that these tremendous events of biblical history are not to be called to mind. They belong to the past. *"Behold, I*

*will do something new, now it will spring forth; Will
you not be aware of it? I will even make a roadway in
the wilderness, rivers in the desert"* (v. 19).

God will do something new and we will know
about it in advance. It will be something new, and
something so significant that it can be compared with
the exodus out of Egypt, but it will be much more
outstanding. It will overshadow all the great things of
the past. There will be a second exodus! Therefore
God is speaking to the nations of the world today and
proclaiming, "I will do something new and all the nations shall know it."

All the promises of God concerning the children of
Israel have either been fulfilled in the past or will be
fulfilled in the future. It is a principle of God to inform
His servants, the prophets, in advance whenever He
wants to do something new in His redemptive plan.
*"Surely the Lord God does nothing, unless He reveals
His secret counsel to His servants the prophets"*
(Amos 3:7). God reveals His secret counsel for His
beloved people to His messengers so that they can be
prepared. *"Declaring the end from the beginning and
from ancient times things which have not been done,
saying, 'My purpose will be established, and I will accomplish all My good pleasure'; calling a bird of prey
from the east, the man of My purpose from a far country. Truly I have spoken; truly I will bring it to pass. I
have planned it, surely I will do it. 'Listen to Me, you
stubborn-minded, who are far from righteousness, it is
not far off; and My salvation will not delay. And I will
grant salvation in Zion, and My glory to Israel'"*
(Isaiah 46:10-13). God is speaking to the world

through many of His servants today and is saying,
"The time has come to bring about the second exodus
of My people."

In Isaiah 43:5-6 we can read a very significant
statement, *"Do not fear, for I am with you; I will
bring your offspring from the east, and gather you
from the west. I will say to the north, 'Give them up!'
and to the south, 'Do not hold them back,' Bring my
sons from afar, and My daughters from the ends of the
earth."* It is interesting that Isaiah wrote these words
over twenty-seven hundred years ago and describes
the bondage of the Jewish people today and God's
desire to set them free.

Concerning the gathering, various expressions
are used in the Bible like, for instance, "lead them
back," "gather them," "do not keep back," and quite
a strong expression, "give them up!" It is quite
remarkable that Isaiah, speaking through the Spirit
of God orders the country of the north, "give them
up!" God knew already at that time about the difficulties His people would have in the "land of the
north." For instance, right now, in 1983, the Soviet
Union has essentially closed all doors so that hardly
any of the two and one-half million Jews are able to
return to the land of promise. But God will provoke
the "land of the north" to let His people go. The
original exodus out of Egypt will seem like just a
shadow of the upcoming dramatic events. No one will
talk about the former exodus anymore because of the
worldwide impact of the final one.

As we continue in the Word of God, we find more
references in regard to the "land of the north." *"Go,*

*and proclaim these words toward the north and say,
'Return, faithless Israel,' declares the Lord; 'I will not
look upon you in anger. For I am gracious,' declares
the Lord: 'I will not be angry forever' "* (Jeremiah
3:12). Many people have traveled in Russia recently.
They have talked to the Jews, showed them the
biblical context about the coming exodus, and urged
them "Prepare yourselves! As it was in the former
days that the people had to leave Egypt in a hurry, so
it will happen to you." I myself have been in Russia
four times on different occasions, talking to Jews in
various places. More than once I have stood in Red
Square in Moscow with raised hands calling out over
the powers of darkness in Russia, "North, give up My
people!"

In fact, God allowed me to see a vision the last
time I was there. I was standing right at the edge of
Red Square, staring at Lenin's tomb where people
were lined up watching the changing of the guard. I
shouted, "Give up, North!" Suddenly I saw such a
crack in the earth that it swallowed Lenin's tomb so
far down in the earth that nobody could any longer
see it. The crack was so great that it went through the
Kremlin, directly behind Lenin's tomb, and it was so
large that no one could cover it up. It had destroyed
the Communist's "god," and people all over Russia
lost their minds and went crazy.

There were those who wanted to cover up the
whole thing to keep it from the people, but they could
not do it. God had exposed one of the idols that the
Russians worshipped.

We read in Jeremiah 3:18, *"In those days the*

house of Judah will walk with the house of Israel, and they will come together from the land of the north to the land that I gave your fathers as an inheritance."

The Word of God describes it in some more detail in Jeremiah 23:3. We read, *"Then I Myself shall gather the remnant of My flock out of all the countries where I have driven them and shall bring them back to their pasture; and they will be fruitful and multiply."*

Again and again we can read in the prophetic scriptures of the Old Testament that God will gather His people out of all the countries where He has driven them. He will bring them back into their homeland. Verses 5 and 6 go on, *"Behold, the days are coming,"* declares the Lord, *"when I shall raise up for David a righteous Branch; and He will reign as king and act wisely and do justice and righteousness in the land. In His days Judah will be saved, and Israel will dwell securely; and this is His name by which He will be called, 'The Lord our righteousness.' "* Here God declares that there will come a day in which He will raise up unto David a "Branch of righteousness," who will reign as king. He will bring justice and righteousness to the earth. This statement certainly pertains to the second coming of Jesus, when He shall come as King and as the Lion of the tribe of Judah, to work righteousness and justice, not as a Lamb led to the slaughter. In His days Judah will be saved, and Israel will dwell securely.

God will bring His Jewish people home to Israel so that when the Messiah appears, they will look on Him *"whom they have pierced"* (Zechariah 12:10). When Jesus returns, He will not come back to a country partly filled with His people, but with all of His people gathered there.

They will see Him! Judah shall be saved and Israel shall finally live securely at that time. The only time when Israel shall live in safety will be when the Messiah returns. We are living presently in Israel and I can assure you that at this time there is no security. Many nations would like to annihilate Israel. God will not allow them to do so. But when the Messiah appears, then there will be safety.

Jeremiah 23:7 continues with the word, "Therefore!" Here we find a number of the events preceding the return of the Messiah and His government. *"Therefore behold, the days are coming,"* *declares the Lord, "when they will no longer say, 'As* *the Lord lives, who brought up the sons of Israel from* *the land of Egypt.' "*

For over three thousand two hundred years the Jewish people have been celebrating the Passover feast. It recalls to their memory how God saved them out of the hands of Pharaoh. At this feast they are reminded of the many miracles God did for them. He led them out of Egypt through the Red Sea, He gave them water out of the rocks, and supplied them with manna. During the day, He led them with a pillar of a cloud and at night with a pillar of fire. Yet Jeremiah proclaims that they will not even speak anymore of these marvelous events. How can this be explained? For thousands of years they have been celebrating the Passover every year because they have been obligated to do it. *"It is a night to be observed for the* *Lord for having brought them out from the land of*

Egypt; this night is for the Lord, to be observed by all the sons of Israel throughout their generations" (Exodus 12:42).

How then can Jeremiah say that they will no longer speak about it? It is difficult for a Jewish mind to comprehend that. This is the most widely celebrated feast for the Jewish people and yet we read in the Bible that we will no longer talk about that. What great event could replace it?

Jeremiah 23:8 explains it, *"but, 'As the Lord lives, who brought up and led back the descendants of the household of Israel from the north land and from all the countries where I had driven them.' Then they will live on their own soil."* Here it is explained that no one will speak anymore about the exodus out of Egypt, but rather about the exodus out of the "land of the north" and all the other countries where God had "driven them."

God knew thousands of years ago that at the end of time His people would be in captivity in the "land of the north," similar to the way in which they had been in captivity in Egypt. There will be a second exodus, the likes of which will not only be comparable to the exodus out of Egypt, but will be so much greater that no one will talk about the first one anymore.

Not only out of Eastern Europe will the Jews go to Israel, but also from America, Argentina, and Australia and out of all the nations of the world. It will begin in the "land of the north" and spread through all the countries of the world. They are coming back into their promised land and will be there when the "Righteous Branch," the King returns.

Therefore thus says the Lord God, "Now I shall restore the fortunes of Jacob, and have mercy on the whole house of Israel; and I shall be jealous for My holy name. And they shall forget their disgrace and all their treachery which they perpetrated against Me, when they live securely on their own land with no one to make them afraid. When I bring them back from the peoples and gather them from the lands of their enemies, then I shall be sanctified through them in the sight of the many nations. Then they will know that I am the Lord their God because I made them go into exile among the nations, and then gathered them again to their own land; and I will leave none of them there any longer. And I will not hide My face from them any longer, for I shall have poured out My Spirit on the house of Israel," declares the Lord God.— Ezekiel 39:25-29

CHAPTER 22

THE PROPHETIC PATTERN OF GOD

God does things prophetically. Before the New Testament came the Old Testament. Before the New Covenant was the Old Covenant. It was the prophetic preparation for the new. Before Jesus came, John the Baptist cried out, "Prepare ye the way of the Lord." This too had been prophetically foretold. God is once again preparing the path for the new. Just as the Old Covenant prepared for the New Covenant, and John the Baptist prepared the way for the ministry of Jesus, so in the last days there will be the preparation for the return of the Lord, the homecoming of the Jewish people to Israel. It will begin in the "land of the north" and spread to every country of the world as God draws all His people back home.

We have already read that God will lift up a standard, or give a sign, for the nations (Isaiah 11:12) by gathering His people. The sign is this final exodus. Will it be a blessing or a curse to the individual coun-

tries when the Jews move through their land? God
will give every nation an opportunity to bless His people, for He wants to see what their attitude is towards
Israel. He told Abraham, *"And I will bless those who
bless you, and the one who curses you I will curse, and
in you all the families of the earth shall be blessed"*
(Genesis 12:3).

The prophet Zechariah at the first commands the
children of Israel to flee out of the country of the
north and then warns every nation about plots to
touch them in order to harm them, " *'Ho there! Flee
from the land of the north,' declares the Lord, 'for I
have dispersed you as the four winds of the heavens,'
declares the Lord. 'Ho, Zion! Escape, you who are living with the daughter of Babylon.' For thus says the
Lord of hosts, 'After glory He has sent me against the
nations which plunder you, for he who touches you,
touches the apple of His eye' "* (Zechariah 2:6-8).

What will be the attitude of your nation toward
the Jews when they return to their promised land?
Only by prayer and intercession will you be able to
determine what the Lord will require of your country.

The Bible says that in the end time there will be a
great falling away. *"And at that time many will fall
away and will deliver up one another and hate one
another"* (Matthew 24:10).

What will trigger that falling away? Could it
begin through those who reject the Jewish people in
the last days? And so God would not spare them?
Romans 11:19-21 gives the answer: *"You will say
then, 'Branches were broken off so that I might be
grafted in.' Quite right, they were broken off for their*

unbelief, but you stand by your faith. Do not be conceited, but fear; for if God did not spare the natural branches, neither will He spare you."

These matters are not to be taken lightly. God will deal severely with those who do not treat His people properly. We need to be clearly informed on these things. *"For I do not want you, brethren, to be uninformed of this mystery, lest you be wise in your own estimation, that a partial hardening has happened to Israel until the fullness of the Gentiles has come in"* (Romans 11:25).

Zechariah 12:2,3 says, *"Behold, I am going to make Jerusalem a cup that causes reeling to all the peoples around; and when the siege is against Jerusalem, it will also be against Judah. And it will come about in that day that I will make Jerusalem a heavy stone for all the peoples; all who lift it will be severely injured. And all the nations of the earth will be gathered against it."*

Even though the Jewish people may be a burden, or a "heavy stone," God will judge the nations according to what they do to help them. He will also judge them if they do anything to hinder or hurt them. It is an immutable law of God that any nation that blesses Israel will in turn be blessed, but anyone who does anything to the people of Israel that would, in effect, be a curse to them, will find that they are bringing a curse also on themselves.

But the warning of God stands, not to touch the "apple of His eye."

As I was preparing myself for a trip around the world in 1983, the Lord gave me a serious message

for all the nations, but especially for Germany and
Finland. It was simply, "Don't be like the land of
Moab!"

When the children of Israel moved out of Egypt,
there were two nations who did not permit them to
pass through their borders and did not give them
bread and water. The one nation was Moab and the
other was Edom. These two nations rejected Israel.
Because they did that, the judgment of God came
upon them later on.

God spoke to my heart, "There are two key nations for the second exodus in Europe: Germany and
Finland. Go to them and declare to these nations that
if they close their borders to the Jews, they will be
like the land of Moab. If that happens, they will have
an adversary greater than any enemy on earth. I, the
God of Israel, will be their adversary. As I have dealt
with Moab, so I will deal with those countries that will
close their borders to My people."

Therefore, burning within me is this message:
"Don't be like the land of Moab!" God loves all people
and He wants to bless them, not destroy them. Go on
your knees before God and pray that the borders of
your nation will be open. Pray for the government
and those who are in authority over you that your nation will stay obedient to the Word of God and help
the Jewish exiles on their way to Israel.

In Exodus 15:11-16 we read, *"Who is like Thee
among the gods, O Lord? Who is like Thee, majestic in
holiness, awesome in praises, working wonders? Thou
didst stretch out Thy right hand, the earth swallowed
them. In Thy lovingkindness Thou has led the people,*

*whom Thou hast redeemed; In Thy strength Thou hast
guided them to Thy holy habitation. The peoples have
heard, they tremble; anguish has gripped the inhabitants of Philistia. Then the chiefs of Edom were
dismayed; the leaders of Moab, trembling grips them;
All the inhabitants of Canaan have melted away. Terror and dread fall upon them; by the greatness of
Thine arm they are motionless as stone; until Thy people pass over, O Lord, until the people pass over whom
Thou hast purchased.*"

If a nation maintains an attitude like that of
Moab, God will make that nation "motionless as
stone." He will lead His people home regardless of
what other nations do, but fear and anguish will come
over those who reject the Jewish people like Moab
did. *"Woe to you Moab! You are ruined, O people of
Chemosh! He has given his sons as fugitives, and his
daughters into captivity"* (Numbers 21:29).

In Numbers 22 we read that the king of Moab
tried to bribe the prophet Balaam to prophesy against
and curse the children of Israel. Because Balak, the
king of Moab, tried to set up a prophet to speak
something other than what God was speaking, his
land was destroyed. There may be people in your
country asserting that the final exodus will never happen and that the scriptures cannot be interpreted in
that way. They are either not understanding the
scriptures or perhaps they are people who do not
believe that God speaks to people today. And yet
Jesus said in John 16:13, *"But when He, the Spirit of
truth, comes, He will guide you into all the truth; for
He will not speak on His own initiative, but whatever*

He hears, He will speak; and He will disclose to you what is to come." The exodus will take place, for the Bible has promised that it will. The nation of Moab was destroyed because they stood against the children of Israel. Do not act as Moab did!

In Jeremiah 31:7-10 we are told what our attitude should be. *"For thus says the Lord, 'Sing aloud with gladness for Jacob, and shout among the chiefs of the nations; proclaim, give praise and say, "O Lord, save Thy people, the remnant of Israel." Behold I am bringing them from the north country, and I will gather them from the remote parts of the earth, among them the blind and the lame, the woman with child and she who is in labor with child, together; a great company, they shall return here. With weeping they shall come, and by supplication I will lead them; I will make them walk by streams of waters, on a straight path in which they shall not stumble; for I am a father to Israel, and Ephraim is My first-born.' Hear the word of the Lord, O nations, and declare in the coastlands afar off, and say, 'He who scattered Israel will gather him, and keep him as a shepherd keeps his flock.'"*

Here is what the nations should do. They should be glad and rejoice over the children of Israel. They should pray, "O Lord, save Your people, the remnant of Israel!" And they should proclaim in their countries that God will gather His people and will protect them. This is our responsibility. Every Christian is able to do this. In this period of growing anti-Semitism, believers will need to stand with the Jewish people and speak well of them.

Believers should never forget that they are the

branches of the wild olive tree that were grafted into the true olive tree because some Jews, not all of them, were disobedient. *"But if some of the branches were broken off, and you, being a wild olive, were grafted in among them and became partaker with them of the rich root of the olive tree,...For just as you once were disobedient to God, but now have been shown mercy because of their disobedience, so these also now have been disobedient, in order that because of the mercy shown to you, they also may now be shown mercy"* (Romans 11:17, 30, 31).

You were able to receive salvation and the grace of God because some of the Jews were disobedient. But not all the Jews were "broken off" (v. 17). We are reminded of Peter, Paul, James, and John and all the other writers of the New Testament who were all Jews with the possible exception of one. The early church was basically a Jewish church. If they had not been faithful, we would not have the message of redemption today. So, according to Romans 11, we should not exalt ourselves over the Jewish people, but show mercy unto them.

Therefore, these words of the Lord have a special significance for us: *"Comfort, O comfort My people,"* says your God. *"Speak kindly to Jerusalem; and call out to her, that her warfare has ended, that her iniquity has been removed, that she has received of the Lord's hand double for all her sins!"* (Isaiah 40:1,2).

PART V

YOUR PART IN GOD'S PLAN

CHAPTER 23

WHAT CAN WE DO?

Many individual Christians in Europe and other places around the world, who are excited about the prophetic revelations about the upcoming exodus, are asking time and again, "When will this happen? What can we do?" I must state clearly and emphatically that I do not know when the exodus will occur. All that I know is that it will take place. The Bible says it will happen. Taking into consideration the increasing persecution of the Jews in Russia, and since our Lord has revealed His specific counsel on the matter independently to many of His servants and confirmed what He has shown me personally, I am sure that our generation will see it come to pass. But, as I have said before, God has never mentioned any date, either to me or to any others that I know.

Why then has God sent this series of prophetic revelations? Surely it is not just for us to be informed and passively await the fulfillment. Whenever God speaks prophetically, He wants to prepare us for an event. His desire is that we, as His co-workers, will cooperate with Him so that His purposes and plans are fulfilled. This is why many are receiving prophetic revelations from the throne of God to the Body of Christ!

It is important for you the reader to prove, or test, all that has been written in this book for yourself. Go into your prayer closet with your Bible and let God speak to your heart concerning His plans for bringing the Jewish people home to Israel. In this way you will not just be taking my word, or the word of others who have had prophetic revelations, but you will be able to hear from the Lord about this matter for yourself. Read the following scriptures and let the Lord speak to you and let the fire of the Holy Spirit seal it in your heart.

Jeremiah 23:3-8	Isaiah 43:16-19, 42:9,
Jeremiah 16:14-16	46:9-13, 48:6
Jeremiah 31:7-10	Deut. 30:3-6
Jeremiah 3:12,18	Jeremiah 30:3,24
Isaiah 43:5-6	Zechariah 2:6-8
Isaiah 11:11-12	Ezekiel 39:25-29

Amos 3:7

At the beginning of 1983, we saw the flight of two million Africans from Nigeria. No one was prepared or in a position to receive or help them. It caused a terrible refugee situation. As God is also the God of history, He is allowing us to graphically see what happens to a people when there is no prophetic preparation for such a great exodus. *"Where there is no vision, the people perish"* (Proverbs 29:18, KJV).

Another exodus of more than two million people is before us. The difference is that this time God has informed the body of Christ in advance and wants them to be prepared to be of help. *"Surely the Lord God does nothing unless He reveals His secret counsel to His servants the prophets"* (Amos 3:7). Does this mean God loves the Jewish people more than the Africans? Do they deserve special preparation? Of course not! Do we deserve our salvation? Of course not! It's because God promised in His Word both our salvation and the safe return of His people to their promised land.

In this end time we need prophetic alertness. The events on the world scene are moving with increasing speed as the end approaches. We need to pay attention to prophetic revelations that must yet be fulfilled. Just as the prophet Daniel found an unfulfilled prophecy during his studies and immediately began to pray and fast, and in that way cooperated with the Lord for the fulfillment (Daniel 9), so we need to pray and ask the Lord to show us how we can cooperate with His plans today.

Once we have received or heard about prophetic revelation, we are called to get involved. We must not remain passive. Our preparation will develop out of what God reveals to us personally. We can be assured that since God has revealed, both in His Word and through prophetic revelations, that the Jewish people will be gathered back into their land, He will also tell each person how to be prepared to help. What God shows to each person individually may be quite different. But if we each do our part, it will all work together to accomplish God's purposes.

There is one thing concerning the exodus that the Lord has laid very clearly on my heart to share wherever I go: The whole plan is the work of the Holy Spirit. Human power and ingenuity will never get the Jews released from Russia. From a human viewpoint, their release looks impossible. Out of natural excitement about God's plan it is easy to let our own ideas get in the way of God's way of doing things. In our enthusiasm we could easily thwart God's purposes. The second exodus is God's plan. It has been revealed by the Holy Spirit and it must continue to be worked out through the leading of the Holy Spirit in order to be successful. Galatians 3:3 warns us, *"Having begun by the Spirit, are you now being perfected by the flesh?"* Each of us must seek to be led by the Holy Spirit as we make ourselves available to the Lord to do whatever He shows us to do.

The preparations we see presently in the Body of Christ are being supernaturally led by the Holy Spirit. It is so utterly fantastic how God has spoken to Christians in so many different countries. They have begun to pray, to share, and to prepare themselves spiritually and in practical ways. No individual person with even the greatest management abilities could have accomplished all of this in such a short period of time, and with such intensity and conviction!

The message will certainly be spread even more widely. And there is always the danger that the more people that hear about it, the more possible it is for people's own opinions, plans, and imaginations to get in the way. We need to be careful so that which has been begun in the Spirit does not eventually end up in the "flesh." The Holy Spirit definitely began it all and He plans to finish it. No man, group, or organization shall be responsible for the accomplishment of the final exodus of the Jews. The glory belongs only to God.

We will not have to organize anything. We do not need lists of names and addresses of those who are preparing places of refuge. The Holy Spirit will lead the Jewish people to the right places at the right time. In fact, you should never give your address or your money to any kind of organization that seeks to take this matter into their own hands! A list of places of refuge could easily fall into wrong hands.

What is important is to go to prayer and ask the Lord personally what you should do! Be open to the exciting experience of having the Lord speak to you and show you His directions. Certainly when you have heard from God, let other Christians, your pastor or the elders, judge the word so you can be sure that there has been no misunderstanding. But you do need to seek the Lord's direction for yourself! If each person will be obedient to God and accomplishes whatever God reveals needs to be done by that person, then we will see the most perfect preparations, because the Holy Spirit will have been the initiator.

We see that *"Unless the Lord builds the house, they labor in vain who build it; unless the Lord guards the city, the watchman keeps awake in vain"* (Psalm 127:1). God will only bless what He starts. He is not obligated to bless our plans. If we will do what He tells us to do, He will take care of the rest.

Sometimes doing "good" things can get in the way of doing God's will. We can discover that it is good to help prepare for the exodus of the Jews out of Russia, but if we just start working for it without first finding out what it is that the Holy Spirit is leading us to do, we can be in danger of building with wood, hay, and straw.

The Apostle Paul warns of this trap in I Corinthians 3:12-15, NIV. *"If any man builds on this foundation using gold, silver, costly stones, wood, hay, or straw, his work will be shown for what it is, because the Day will bring it to light. It will be revealed with fire, and the fire will test the quality of each man's work. If what he has built survives, he will receive his reward. If it is burned up, he will suffer loss; he himself will be saved, but only as one escaping through the flames."*

It has been my heart's desire to walk daily with the Lord, constantly seeking the Holy Spirit's guidance in these matters. I do not want to stand before the Lord and see that all I have done for Him is burned up because it was not what He had led me to do, but rather my own idea. It's the motivation that counts. Be sure that what you do is being prompted by the Holy Spirit.

I would like to suggest seven practical guidelines for prayer. The victory will first have to be won in prayer before it will be accomplished on this earth. We know for sure that our battle is not *"against flesh and blood, but against the rulers, against the powers, against the world forces of this darkness, against the spiritual forces of wickedness in the heavenly places"* (Ephesians 6:12). We must battle in prayer against these powers of the unseen world. We have the promise of victory! But that victory is manifested as we pray.

Earnestly pray about this matter. Spend time with the Lord. He will show you the guidelines He wants you to pursue so that you can move ahead in His plan.

The seven guidelines have been derived from the exodus out of Egypt. We know that the second exodus will have some parallels to the first one. It does not mean that God will do exactly the same in Russia as He did in Egypt, but we certainly can find spiritual strategy in it. As in the times of the first exodus, we will need a type of ministry like that of Moses that will move in prayer with the authority of the Lord against the spiritual forces over the Soviet Union, commanding them to let God's people go. We must pray that many people will be willing to be used in a ministry of Moses to break the spiritual powers of darkness that hold God's people prisoners.

In the vision that I had in 1974 where God showed me how He would bring the Jewish people out of Russia, I saw that God had raised up men with ministries as great as and even greater than that of Moses. They proclaimed to the authorities, "Let My people go!" Then, in the vision, God judged the Soviet Union with such devastation that they could not wait for the Jews to get out of the country. Then I also saw ministries like that of Moses that were leading them out of Russia on the road to freedom.

Later, with some of the insights of Pastor Kjell Sjoberg from Sweden, we saw the need for a variety of ministries patterned after the total ministry of Moses that would help to prepare for the great exodus. Jointly we prepared the seven points that follow.

1. Pray for God to raise up people with a ministry of Moses with knowledge about the Soviet Union.

In Acts 7:22, we read that Moses had been educated in all the wisdom of the Egyptians and was mighty in words and deeds. Moses knew the culture and the ways of the Egyptians very well. In the same way, we need people who are called of God and have the knowledge about the culture and the way of life in the Soviet Union.

Keep yourself informed about the political and economic developments in Russia. Follow very closely what the media is saying about the situation of the Jews in the Soviet Union. God has been speaking to some people who already have a vast knowledge about the Soviet Union to be available to help with the Jewish exodus out of Russia. God may speak to others to begin to study about the Russian culture. Many are saying that news articles and broadcasts about the USSR now catch their attention since they know about God's plans to eventually bring that communist country to its knees in order to secure the release of the Jewish people.

Pray for people to be motivated to learn the Russian language. It will be so important that there are people in every community where the Russian Jewish refugees stay that can speak at least some Russian. In my own experience in traveling through many nations, I know how essential it is to find someone who can communicate with me in my own language. The very fact that a person has made the attempt to know the Russian language will speak volumes about the person's love for the Jewish refugees.

God has already been speaking to believers all over the world to learn Russian. I believe He wants to raise up many more people who will be prepared to interpret for the benefit of the refugees. Imagine the possibilities there will be to share your knowledge of Jesus with them. They will come, having been spiritually starved for all or most of their lives. How good it will be to be able to communicate to them the Bread of Life.

> Read: Hebrews 11:23-29
>   Acts 7:22-38

2. Pray for God to raise up people with a ministry of Moses to confront the government of the Soviet Union.

We need men like Moses who, at the command of God, will actually go to the government of the Soviet Union and tell the authorities to "Let My people go!"

Why did the Soviet Union want to close its borders? Why was the Iron Curtain built? Why do they persecute Jews, Christians, and dissidents? Spiritually, it's because the goal of the Satanic powers over the nation is to keep people in the darkness of atheism and from knowing the Way of Salvation. The Apostle Paul said, *"...the god of this world has blinded the minds of the unbelieving, that they might not see the light of the gospel of the glory of Christ, who is the image of God"* (II Corinthians 4:4).

Most of the Jewish people in the Soviet Union are well educated, being doctors, scientists, teachers, engineers, etc. To let these people go would deprive the nation of a rich resource. Soviet pride would also be wounded if so many educated people were able to leave. There is also the fear by the Russian authorities that many people would speak out against the injustices going on inside that nation, like Solschenizyn and Shifrin have. Especially now, as the Soviet Union is permitting hardly any of the Jewish people to leave, we must effectively pray and raise our voices in behalf of the Jews. We need people who will go boldly to the authorities in the Soviet Union and demand liberty for the Jewish people.

It is also important to mobilize world opinion. This can be done, for instance, through demonstrations before the Russian embassies and through letters to our government, requesting that they act positively on the situation of the Jews in the Soviet Union.

There are already some organized efforts such as the Mordecai Outcry and the Esther Fast, that are making an impact. Also, the committee for Soviet Jewry* and other Jewish organizations are effective-

---

*The main organization to contact is: The Union of Councils for Soviet Jews, Suite 402, 1411 K St. N.W., Washington, D.C. 20005, U.S.A.

ly informing the public about the situation of the Russian Jews. They also publish lists of political prisoners, encouraging people to write to them to let them know that people care.

> Read: Exodus 3:10
>   Exodus 4:10-13
>   Exodus 5:1

3. Pray for God to raise up people with the ministry of Moses to prepare the Russian Jews to leave.

Moses did not only go to Pharoah, he also went to the Israelites and prepared them to be ready to leave Egypt in a hurry. He gave them instructions for the exodus. Even at this point many have gone into the Soviet Union with this message to get ready to leave. Some of the Jewish people have had receptive ears, but some have rejected the idea. I personally have been in Russia four times and have talked with Jews in the synagogues, in their homes, on the streets, at the beach, and on trains. I have shared the message with them and exhorted them to get ready to leave.

I personally found that the elders among the Jewish people in the Soviet Union who were knowledgeable of the scriptures believed what I had to say. "When will this exodus happen?" they would ask. They are eager to get out. *"Then Moses and Aaron went and assembled all the elders of the sons of Israel; and Aaron spoke all the words which the Lord had spoken to Moses. He then performed the signs in the sight of the people. So the people believed; and when they heard that the Lord was concerned about the sons of Israel and that He had seen their affliction, then they bowed low and worshipped"* (Exodus 4:29-31).

But I also found there those who preferred the security of their job, home, and the little amount that they had, who rejected our message of the coming exodus. They would react by saying, "You're a fanatic, a political activist! You're wanting to cause us harm!" They were afraid of more political pressure. *"When they left Pharoah's presence, they met Moses and Aaron as they were waiting for them. And they said to them, 'May the Lord look upon you and judge you, for you have made us odious in Pharaoh's sight and in the sight of his servants, to put a sword in their hand to kill us' "* (Exodus 5:20-21).

Pray that the Russian Jews will have open hearts to respond to the message of deliverance. Pray for those who are carrying the message inside Russia, that they might be guided by the Holy Spirit to those who are ready to hear. Pray both for the protection of those who take the message and for those who hear it.

> Read: Exodus 3:7-9
>   Exodus 3:13 & 18
>   Exodus 4:29-31

4. Pray for God to raise up a ministry of Moses for the spiritual battle.

This is no game; we are in the midst of a real battle with the forces of darkness in the spiritual world. Satan wants to destroy people; God wants to set them free!

Moses stood in the spiritual battle with the gods

of Egypt. All the plagues that came over Egypt were directed against the gods that the Egyptians worshipped.

It may seem incredible to us today but it is a fact that they worshipped over eighty gods of various types and descriptions. God chose ten representative plagues with which to judge all the idols they worshipped. For instance, the Egyptians worshipped serpents and so the rod of Moses was turned into a more powerful serpent that devoured Pharaoh's. They worshipped the Nile River, and so God turned it into blood. They worshipped the sun god and so the sun was darkened. They worshipped frogs and were forbidden to kill them. So God gave them a few. Imagine frogs everywhere, in the streets, in their houses, in their beds. They couldn't step anywhere without squishing them. They also worshipped the locusts and flies and so God sent them more than they could handle. God's judgment was manifested in the things that the Egyptians had been worshipping as gods.

The confrontations with Pharaoh and his magi cians were power confrontations with the demonic spirits in Egypt. Even though Satan's power here on this earth is extensive, God's power is much greater. He wants to demonstrate His power today in and through believers who have a pure heart.

We need to know what idols are being worshipped in the Soviet Union today. Naturally the Russians would say that they are not worshipping anything at all. They maintain that they are atheists and that there is no God. And yet, everytime I cross the border into Russia, the first question the guard asks me is, "Do you have any Bibles?" I cannot help but wonder why they are so concerned about a book about God getting into their country if, as they say, there is no God! But they are worshipping many things. Anything that is being more honored than God is an idol. Against these God will stretch forth His hand. What could possibly be the gods of Russia? Could it be their science, their military power, their pride, greed, hatred, their love for their motherland, alcohol, deception, witchcraft, sadism, their atheism?

People are needed who know how to do spiritual warfare. It is necessary to discern which idols they worship, define the areas of demonic activity that accompany them, and move out in spiritual warfare against them in the name and power of Jesus. We also need to pray that God will bring down His judgment on the gods the Russians worship.

"While the Egyptians were burying all their first-born whom the Lord had struck down among them. The Lord had also executed judgments on their gods" (Numbers 33:4).

> Read: Exodus 7-11
>   II Corinthians 10:4,5
>   Matthew 11:12
>   Ephesians 6:19

5. Pray for God to raise up a ministry of Moses to help prepare those nations through which the Jews will move.

It is very important that the nations be prepared

to accept the Jewish refugees so that borders will not be closed when the exodus takes place. We remember how the two nations, Edom and Moab, denied the children of Israel any help and resisted their attempt to move through their country. Therefore, God had to deal harshly with these countries. This serious warning pertains to us: "Don't be like the land of Moab!"

We need to pray that hearts and homes will be prepared to receive the Jewish refugees. At the present time, we do not know how governments, the public, the churches, and individuals will react toward such a mass exodus of the Jews through their country. It will be an inconvenience, to say the least. Imagine thousands of people suddenly coming into your community with nowhere to sleep and nothing to eat.

Will voices of rejection be in the majority or will it be the voices of those who help and give emergency aid for these refugees as they continue on their exodus from Russia to Israel?

We need to teach in our churches about the place of Israel in the prophetic Word. We need to watch that the Body of Christ will not be poisoned by anti-Semitic propaganda. When the exodus occurs, it is not likely that the government agencies alone will be able to handle the situation. If the tide of public opinion moves against the giving of emergency aid to the Jews, will the churches and individual Christians be prepared to help?

There is a dangerous social and political bomb in the coming events.

"Anti-Zionism" and "anti-Israel" are only different words for "anti-Semitism." But these terms are being used more widely today in order to attack the Jewish people. The spirit behind this is Satanic, all a part of his plan to discredit and destroy God's people and to thwart God's plan to get them back to Israel.

What are the attitudes of the nations toward Israel? How many of them are backing the nation in its struggle to survive in a world that has become hostile to it?

We need to pray especially for those who govern. *"First of all, then, I urge that entreaties and prayers, petitions and thanksgivings, be made on behalf of all men, for kings and all who are in authority, in order that we may lead a tranquil and quiet life in all godliness and dignity"* (I Timothy 2:1,2).

> Read: Numbers 20:14-21
>   Joshua 2:8-13
>   Genesis 41:15-36

6. Pray for God to raise up a ministry of Moses with the knowledge of the traveling routes.

God prepared Moses for forty years in the desert so that he would know how to live in the desert and how to travel in the desert. We, too, need people who know the roads for the Jews to travel on in both eastern and western Europe during the exodus.

In Jeremiah 31:21 we find that there is a "highway" that God is preparing. *"Set up for yourself roadmarks, place for yourself guideposts; direct your mind to the highway, the way by which you went. Return, O virgin of Israel, return to these your cities."*

God has a plan in the heavenlies for the highways by which His people will be led back to Israel. We need to pray for revelation of this information. Some of these routes have already been revealed. God has been speaking to various people about His specific plans. But we don't have the whole picture as yet. Pray that all of those who need to know about the routes will: 1) be open to hear from God on these matters, 2) be in contact with those who have received the relevant information, and 3) be led by the Holy Spirit as they travel to freedom.

The Lord has shown me that there are certain cities that must not be traveled through. For whatever reasons God has, we know that they are valid. Pray that people will be warned or prevented in some way from going to or through these places. We are warned in the scriptures not to be in cities that are completely under the influence of demon powers. *"And he cried out with a mighty voice, saying 'Fallen, fallen is Babylon the great! And she has become a dwelling place of demons and a prison of every unclean spirit, and a prison of every unclean and hateful bird. For all the nations have drunk of the wine of the passion of her immorality, and the kings of the earth have committed acts of immorality with her, and the merchants of the earth have become rich by the wealth of her sensuality.' And I heard another voice from heaven, saying, 'Come out of her, my people, that you may not participate in her sins and that you may not receive of her plagues'"* (Revelation 18:2-4).

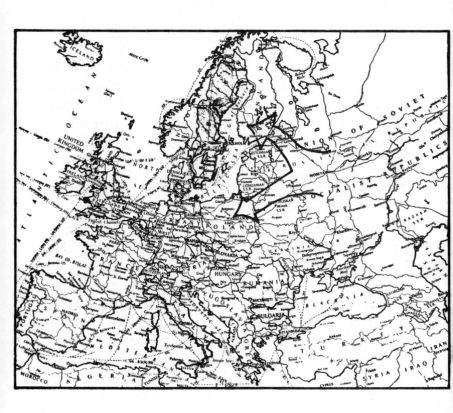

Steve Lightle's two visions (in 1974 and 1980) indicated that there would be two main routes by which the Jewish people would come out of the Soviet Union. The major movement of the exodus will be westward through Poland, Germany, and Holland. The second route will be through the Finnish border.

God is also preparing cities of refuge. These are the places God wants His people to go to. We read about such places in both the Old and New Testaments. In Joshua, we see that these cities are places to "flee to." *"Speak to the sons of Israel, saying, 'Designate the cities of refuge, of which I spoke to you through Moses' "* (Joshua 20:2).

In Revelation 12:6 we see an example of how God prepares a place ahead of time. *"And the woman fled into the wilderness where she had a place prepared by God, so that there she might be nourished for one thousand two hundred and sixty days."*

In the last ten years, God has permitted me to travel hundreds of thousands of kilometers throughout eastern and western Europe. Even though it was my work that necessitated my going throughout Europe, I knew deep inside of me that there was a greater purpose for it all. Now I see that it was part of God's plan so that I would be knowledgeable of the possible traveling routes for the great exodus that is to come.

Many other Christians are also being led to travel in Europe and to become familiar with the routes. Pray that God will lead others to be available to travel and get to know them as well.

Read: Isaiah 35:8
           Jeremiah 31:21
           Isaiah 62:10
           Isaiah 43:19

7. Pray for God to raise up a ministry of Moses to bring the Word of God to the Jews.

As the children of Israel moved out of Egypt in that first great exodus, Moses gave them the word of God. Moses went up the mountain to seek direction from God and God gave him the words of His Covenant and the Ten Commandments to give to the people.

As the Jews move out of Russia, they, too, will need direction. God wants to give it to them. He wants them to have His Word so that they will know His plans for them. Wouldn't it be wonderful if every Christian home in western Europe had some Russian Bibles on hand? Then, when the Jews travel through, a Russian Bible could be put into their hands and God will be able to reveal Himself and His plan to them through His Word.

For those who don't know the Russian language, a photocopy of the letter printed in this book can be made and given with the Russian Bible. This letter will welcome the Jews in Russian and in Hebrew and encourage them to return to the land of their forefathers. Many European homes already have Russian Bibles. Thousands of Russian Bibles are still available to be distributed. Pray that they will get into the homes where they will be needed. Most of the Russian Jews will have little or no knowledge of their Jewish heritage. Remember they have been living in a country that has denied them the right to attend synagogue without fear of penalty, to have synagogue schools, to study Hebrew, or to pursue knowledge of their culture.

As a result of this lack of knowledge, they will likely be more open to receive the Word of God. They will be eager to learn about their background and heritage. They will know that their being Jewish has been the reason for their persecution and will want to know why this has been so. They will welcome the opportunity to read the Russian Bibles that are given to them.

Pray that there will be Bibles available wherever the Jewish refugees pass through on this second, and greatest exodus.

Read: Exodus 19
Exodus 20:1-17

These seven guidelines for prayer are very important for the preparations that are necessary for the release of the Russian Jews out of the grip of the Satanic powers over the Soviet Union. Let God show you how He wants you to intercede. Become familiar with what God's Word says about the release of His people. Be obedient if the Holy Spirit shows you to make any particular preparations.

If each of us is faithful to seek the Lord's guidance and to do all that He shows us to do, then the Lord will certainly "prepare the way!"

CHAPTER 24

THE WAYS OF GOD

There is a scripture that God has burned within my heart: *"He made known His ways to Moses, His acts to the sons of Israel"* (Psalms 103:7). There is a big difference between the acts of God and the ways of God. So many people today want to see the acts and miracles of God. I love to see them too. I'm not against them. As a matter of fact, I believe every believer should be seeing them happen. But it is a matter of what is most important.

When the children of Israel came out of Egypt, they saw all the *acts* of God. They saw the plagues, they saw the deliverance out of the hand of Pharoah, they saw the Red Sea open up, they saw the pillar of cloud by day and the pillar of fire by night, they saw the bitter water turned sweet, they saw the water come out of the rock, and they saw God's supernatural provision as they gathered the manna off the ground and ate the quail. Yet every person, except two, that came out of Egypt and saw the acts of God, died in the wilderness. They never went into the Promised Land.

But God revealed His *ways* to Moses. And he was the one who did the acts. He was the one God used to bring forth the plagues, to open the sea, to bring water out of the rock, and all the other miraculous things. So, the key to the miraculous and to the acts of God is knowing the *ways of God*.

But so many people want to skip the discipline and price you have to pay to learn the ways of God. It is not easy. It takes a willingness to die to self and to want God's ways more than anything else. The cry in my heart that has become more intense over the years is, "God, teach me Your ways!"

In Proverbs 16:25 we see that, *"There is a way which seems right to a man, but its end is the way of death."* We cannot trust our own human judgment. We are fallible. Something can seem so logical, so right, so expedient to us, and yet it may have nothing at all to do with the will of God or His ways.

Take, for instance, the story in the sixth chapter of II Samuel about David's attempt to bring the Ark of the Lord up to Jerusalem. It was a good thing to do, but he did it the wrong way — and it caused another man's death. Uzzah tried to steady the Ark when it nearly tipped over. No man can touch God's glory and power with his hands and live. Uzzah was struck down.

But it wasn't completely Uzzah's fault, it was also David's. Instead of seeking God's way to carry the Ark, he used a new cart to move the Ark, as the

Philistines had. He copied the world's system to accomplish his goal. Now it was a valid goal to get the Ark back to Jerusalem — but even a valid goal must be accomplished in God's way.

One thing I don't want to be guilty of is using a new cart. I know God plans to bring the Jews back to Israel from out of the country of the north (the Soviet Union), but it must be done God's way.

Some are saying, "Let's get an organization going! Let's take advantage of all the modern technology and systems available to us. Let's get a strong leader, and public relations people, and mailing lists, and a computer, and raise money. We can hold huge meetings and start a magazine and get on television, then we'll see that the Jews are released from Russia."

But remember how Uzzah reached out and touched the Ark of the Lord and died. The awesome fear of the Lord is in my heart concerning this whole thing because it's so close to the heart of God — the Jews coming out of the Soviet Union and going back to Israel along with the Jews from all over the world. If somebody reaches out to touch this, they could be killed, or cause the death of someone else.

It was David's idea to bring the Ark of the Covenant to Jerusalem. He wasn't killed; it was one of the men working together with him that was killed. This makes me want to be very responsible before God so that I don't cause the death of someone else. If I were to go and try to get the release of the Russian Jews accomplished with man's ways, instead of God's ways, what would happen to the people that would be working with me? I could literally or spiritually cause the death of someone else. I don't want that upon my hands.

Anyone who tries to organize the exodus of the Jews or reaches out to touch what is so dear to the heart of God could suffer death. We cannot *cart* about God's glory. It's impossible for us to handle it with our hands. One man said a cart is made out of "boards" and "big wheels." How many people have died spiritually because they've gotten involved with a religious organization and found out when they got inside that their ways were not God's ways? And they fell by the wayside.

We don't need an organization. God has already spoken to the hearts of hundreds of people to prepare for all the things that will be needed. If God can guide people to pray over specific portions of borders, He can certainly direct the Jewish people by His Holy Spirit during the exodus. We don't need computers and mailing lists; we need God!

David stopped when he saw that he had made a mistake and asked this question, *"How can the Ark of the Lord come to me?"* (v. 9).

And the question I keep asking the Lord is, "How do You want the Jews to come out of the Soviet Union and from around the world? What is Your way?" I know we cannot in any way, shape, or form depend upon the ways of the world. It's going to be God's ways that we need to understand.

When David found out God's way to bring the Ark of the Lord to Jerusalem, he did it God's way. The Scripture says he brought the Ark to Jerusalem with gladness (v. 12). When we do something God's way, we'll not have sorrow, we'll do it gladly. Joy is realized when we do it God's way! That's what David found out, and he came dancing with all his might before the Ark of the Lord.

It may not be a fast trip but it gets accomplished. It's done in God's time and in God's way.

When David learned of God's way to get the goal accomplished, he sacrificed, he sacrificed, and he sacrificed! When we read the account in II Samuel 6:12, 13, we find he took six steps and then he stopped and sacrificed. You know, that's a pretty slow trip. But he never saw the accomplishment of his goal at all when he tried to do it his own way. But when he went about it God's way, he recognized that he, as a man, could only take six steps — which is the number of man — and then he had to stop and sacrifice. Then God would empower him to take the next six steps.

God builds *"Order on order, order on order, line on line, line on line, a little here, a little there"* (Isaiah 28:13). David arrived at the goal doing it God's way.

And what is the sacrifice that is necessary for the believer today? Thanksgivng and praise and joy. It's also the sacrifice of dying to our plans, our own will, and our own way. It's taking all the things that we want to do and putting them aside and choosing that God's will be done.

How can this happen? There's only one way and that is daily picking up our cross and living a crucified life. It's dying to self and living for God. Dying to self also means that we take the time to pray, to fast, and to seek God's will. There is indeed a *price to pay.*

What happened to Jesus when He picked up His cross? He was crucified! Yet Jesus said, *"If anyone wishes to come after Me, let him deny himself, and take up his cross, and follow Me"* (Matthew 16:24). This is God's way. It is the only way to walk through this life.

Jesus goes on to warn, *"For what will a man be profited, if he gains the whole world, and forfeits his soul? Or what will a man give in exchange for his soul?"* (v. 26). It's so important that our motives are to follow God's will in all things. None of our personal goals or plans amount to anything compared to accomplishing God's purposes and plans.

Jesus said, *"I am the way, and the truth, and the life; no one comes to the Father, but through Me"* (John 14:6).

While it's a wonderful verse for salvation, it's much more than that. When you know Jesus intimately, you're going to find the truth. Just once? No. He will lead us into all truth in every area of our life. An ongoing process begins as we surrender our life and repent of our sinful, self-centered nature and accept Jesus and His forgiveness and new life. Then as we begin to follow Him, He begins to build His life into us. It's a way of life! It's letting Him become the way, the truth, and the life in us.

One reason Jesus had to come to be "the way," is because so few people could see the ways of God. Man always wants to put everything into a nice little uniform box, or make a plan, or have a computerized program so all you do is press the buttons. Then man doesn't have to depend on God in given situations. We tend to trust in our past experiences and past victories, instead of trusting in the Lord and seeing His ways being accomplished each day. Over and over in the Bible God teaches us His ways, wanting us to walk in His paths so that He can guide our steps. A person that walks in God's way delights in that way.

I never used to be one who wanted to learn the ways of God: I just wanted to see His acts. I wanted to see the dead raised, I wanted to see people come out of wheel chairs, I wanted to see the blind receive their sight. I still do, very much! But I found out that the motives I had in my heart for all that were not right. God wants to first teach me His ways. He wants me to develop that intimate communion with Him that is so necessary for genuine spiritual growth. Then He gets the glory for whatever He may do through me.

God has been speaking very much to my heart about all of this. The children of Israel knew the *acts* of God, but Moses knew the *ways* of God. Whether it's in my own personal life, or whether it's concerning something on a worldwide scale that God wants to do, I first need to learn the ways of God. His ways are so essential.

The most important thing I have learned to do in order to learn God's ways is to get into the Word of God and ask God to teach me His ways. It is something that just cries from the depths of my heart. Great is my desire to learn the ways of God! And God has to teach this. It comes from reading the Word and through prayer. Then the next step is obedience. It's not just enough to find out what His ways are, we must also follow them.

I generally find God's way is absolutely the opposite of the way I would do it. But I'm the one who must change.

When the Ark of the Covenant was left at Obed-edom's house, his whole family was blessed (II Samuel 6:11). God wants to bless us, not hurt us. But if we violate God's Word, then we open ourselves to the judgment of God. And as we are coming closer to the last days, there's just not going to be room for people to do things with wrong motives. Consequently I have to constantly bring myself before God and have Him check my motives. It's simply being honest with myself before God and seriously seeking the face of God so that He can show me what's in my heart.

God is going to continue to raise up people for various tasks in this plan of His for the second exodus. There may be those who get jealous and say, "Well, why did God have this person do that?" or "Why does that person get to do this?" We cannot judge. Look at what happened to David's wife, Michal. She was critical and full of pride. We must be very careful when we see God using other people, that we don't become jealous or envious and begin to speak out against them, because we could dry up spiritually like she did. Michal never bore children because she lived a life of jealousy and pride. If we become jealous when we see God using someone in a particular way, we won't bear fruit in our lives either.

Each person must seek to find out what their part is in God's plan, not look to see what someone else is doing. If each person does whatever God shows them to do, we'll see the whole exodus come to pass in God's time and in God's way.

Paul gave us a graphic example of the need for everyone to do their part in God's plan. In I Corinthians 12:12-27, he explains how just as the human body needs each part to function well in order for the whole body to be healthy, so we--as members of the Body of Christ--need to be doing our part so that the Body of Christ will be healthy and functioning properly.

We can't get our eyes on what others are doing or not doing. The important thing is to "see" what the Lord wants us to do.

After Jesus had told Peter how he was going to be imprisoned and die, Peter immediately wanted to know what was going to happen to John. But it was none of Peter's business and Jesus rebuked him with *"What is that to you? You follow Me!" (John 21:22).*

God speaks to us in many ways. He can use a mighty rushing wind, He can use the sound of many waters, a trumpet, a still inner voice, an audible voice, a word of knowledge, or a word of prophecy. He can speak to us through His Word. And I suspect we hear the voice of the Lord much more than we realize. The Holy Spirit *"bears witness with our spirit"* (Romans 8:16), and all of a sudden we just know what God has said.

In Isaiah 55:8-9 it says: *"For my thoughts are not your thoughts, Neither are your ways My ways," declares the Lord. "For as the heavens are higher than the earth, So are My ways higher than your ways, And my thoughts than your thoughts."*

God's thoughts are higher than ours but nowhere in the Bible does it say we cannot come to know God's thoughts or His ways. We can learn them through reading the Word of God. Then we can see how true the world's ways are contrary to God's ways.

The world says, "Get all you can for yourself. Look our for number one!"

But Jesus says, *"Give, and it will be given to you; good measure, pressed down, shaken together, running over, they will pour into your lap"* (Luke 6:38).

The world says, "It's my life and I'm going to live it just the way I please."

Jesus says, *"For whoever wishes to save his life shall lose it; but whoever loses his life for My sake shall find it"* (Matthew 16:25).

The world says, "Judge the faults of others, cut them down to size if necessary, to keep them in their place."

Jesus says, *"Do not judge lest you be judged"* (Matthew 7:1).

The world says, "None of that Christian stuff for me, I don't want to live in bondage to do's and don't's."

Jesus says, *"For my yoke is easy, and My load is light"* (Matthew 11:30).

The world says, "There are a lot of things that I couldn't possibly do."

Jesus says, *"All things are possible to him who believes"* (Mark 9:23).

Our minds have to be renewed. The old worldly thinking has to be washed out and God's ways washed in. The apostle Paul tells us, *"...be renewed in the spirit of your mind, and put on the new self, which in the likeness of God has been created in righteousness and holiness of the truth"* (Ephesians 4:23, 24). He also explains that believers are cleansed *"by the washing of water with the word"* (Ephesians 5:26).

Paul said in Philippians 2:5, *"Let this mind be in you, which was also in Christ Jesus"* (KJV). If we can have the mind of Christ, it stands to reason we can also have His thoughts and thereby come to know His ways. His thoughts are much higher than ours. But instead of trying to bring God down to us, we should allow God to bring us up to His way of thinking by reading His Word so that we'll understand His ways.

Since the Lord is dealing with the Body of Christ today by purifying and refining it, we should expect to see an increase in signs and wonders. Because of the vision that the Lord showed me of the ministry of Moses to help the Jews come out of Russia, I know that God is going to release an outpouring of the gift of miracles. Stop and consider that Moses was just a *servant* of God and yet he did miracles that have astounded the world even to this day. But we are *sons* and *daughters* of God and how much more God wants to use us in the gift of miracles, in the gifts of healing, and in all the gifts of the Holy Spirit. How God wants to use us! His heart is ready to pour out so much, if we are willing, purified vessels.

But how many people are prepared in the ways of God to be able to handle the acts of God? All the power of God is potentially within the life of every single believer. But God doesn't release it until we come to a place that He knows and we know that He's changed us enough that we're able to walk in it and handle the power of God moving through our lives.

The anointing of God is a very powerful thing.

David was anointed when Samuel poured a horn of oil over his head. After David received his anointing, there was someone who wanted to kill him with a spear. That often also comes with the anointing. So many people are looking for the power of God without responsibility. But I believe God is calling us to responsibility and then we will receive His power.

I'm talking about the miraculous power that Jesus spoke of in John 14:12: *"Truly truly, I say unto you, he who believes in Me, the works that I do shall he do also; and greater works than these shall he do; because I go to the Father."* Jesus said that we would do the very works that He did. I really believe it's going to happen with every believer that walks with integrity and pureness of heart, being led by the Holy Spirit. We're eventually going to see the whole Body of Christ walking that way. I think that's what God wants for every one of us, not for just some super stars or super heroes, but everyone. But we've got to pay the price, and that's to allow God to deal with and purify our lives.

We need to learn His ways instead of just running after miracles and signs. Signs are supposed to follow us: *"And these signs shall follow them that believe..."* (Mark 16:17 KJV). We don't follow the signs. And I find so many people wanting to run to where the signs are instead of every believer having signs following them. But learning God's ways has become the greatest desire of my heart. *How* God does things is more important than *that* He does things.

We are ultimately involved in more than just

Jews coming out of the Soviet Union and from around the world to return to Israel. We are involved in the prophetic preparation for the return of the Messiah. That's our focal point. It's so much greater than everything else put together.

This is important for people to see that we must not just get caught up with the act of the Jews coming out of the Soviet Union. The return of the Jews to Israel is one of the great prophetic signs of the return of the Messiah. Everyone can be involved in prayer and/or in preparations. But it's going to be done the way God wants it to be done.

APPENDIX

THE POPULATION NUMBER OF THE JEWS
IN THE SOVIET UNION
In the book there have been a variety of reports
and quotations about the number of Jews in the
Soviet Union. One reason for this is that different
people have given statistics based on different years.
On the other hand, several organizations give dif-
ferent numbers.

The *American Jewish Yearbook* from 1980 indicates there are 2.678 million Jews living in the
USSR. Other sources suggest 2.15 million. There are
groups who work among Jews in the Soviet Union
that state that there are between three to five million
Jews. The Moscow census of 1979 showed that only
1.8 million Jews live in the USSR. This number certainly can be doubted, for Moscow, Leningrad, Kiev,
and Odessa alone have almost one million Jews. Also
many people may not have been willing to reveal their

Jewish identity in a Russian census since to do so would automatically put them in a position to be persecuted. Many census takers do not bother to examine "internal passports" or otherwise verify declarations.

Most experts on Soviet Jewry seem to agree that it is likely that there are about two and one-half to three million Jews in Russia at the present time. These are the figures that have been used generally in this book.

At any rate, it is interesting to note that there are almost as many Jews living in Russia as in the nation of Israel. Opportunity, indeed, for a very large exodus of Russian Jews. And if they all emigrate to Israel, it would immediately double Israel's population.

According to the Israel Information Center in Jerusalem, "over 36% of the Jews live in three cities, Moscow, Leningrad, and Kiev. In all, 97.6% live in towns or cities." This makes the Jews an almost exclusively urban nationality.

JEWISH WORLD POPULATION
According to the *American Jewish Yearbook* of 1980, the largest Jewish population groups are as follows:

COUNTRIES

USA.........................5,781,000
Israel......................3,135,000
SOVIET UNION 2,678,000

```
France ....................... 650,000
Great Britain ................. 410,000
Canada ....................... 305,000
Argentina..................... 300,000
Brazil ....................... 150,000
South Africa.................. 118,000
Hungary....................... 80,000
Iran.......................... 80,000
Australia/New Zealand ........ 70,000
```

CITIES

```
New York ................... 1,998,000
Los Angeles ................. 455,000
Tel Aviv/Jaffa .............. 394,000
Paris ....................... 300,000
Philadelphia ................ 295,000
MOSCOW ...................... 285,000
London ...................... 280,000
Jerusalem.................... 272,000
Chicago ..................... 253,000
Miami ....................... 225,000
Haifa........................ 210,000
Lyons ....................... 200,000
KIEV ........................ 170,000
Boston ...................... 170,000
LENINGRAD ................... 165,000
Washington, D.C. ............ 160,000
ODESSA ...................... 120,000
Montreal..................... 115,000
Toronto ..................... 115,000
```

EMIGRATION PERMISSION FROM 1970 TO 1983

```
1970 ..............................4,235
1971 .............................13,022
1972 .............................31,681
1973 .............................34,733
1974 .............................20,628
1975 .............................13,221
1976 .............................14,261
1977 .............................16,736
1978 .............................28,864
1979 .............................51,320
1980 .............................21,471
1981 ..............................9,447
1982 ..............................2,688
1983 ..............................1,200*
```

* (Projected from January-April figures.)

THE HELSINKI AGREEMENT*

The signing in Helsinki on August 1, 1975, of the Final Act of the Conference on Security and Cooperation in Europe by thirty-three European States, the USA, and Canada, represented an accord between East and West that was hailed, not least by the spokesmen of eastern Europe, as an event of the greatest importance and of international and humanitarian significance.

The Conference also discussed freer movement of people, ideas, and information between East and

West. Cooperation in humanitarian fields was therefore an essential element of its conclusions.

The British Prime Minister, Harold Wilson, in his Helsinki speech, said that the Conference's work "will be judged by how the spirit (of 'live and let live') is reflected in the lives of ordinary families, by such issues as the reunification of families, the marriages of citizens of different States, the greater possibilities of travel..."

The Helsinki document does not use the term ' emigration" but speaks of "reunification of families." In fact, the emigration of Soviet Jews is based on the concept that it is facilitating the reunification of families, as is evident from the fact that, as a first step in the emigration process, the applicant must submit a written certified invitation affidavit (vyzov) from relatives abroad to join them.

The Helsinki Declaration contains:
- Pledges to facilitate freer movement in general;
- Specific provisions on "reunification of families;"
- Reaffirmation of other international in struments — the Universal Declaration of Human Rights, the Convention against Race Discrimination, and the Human Rights Covenants —which ordain freedom to leave one's country.

Applications to emigrate to Israel are also covered by the special section in the Helsinki Final

Act on "Questions relating to Security and Cooperation in the Mediterranean." This contains an explicit declaration that the Helsinki principles will be applied to "the relations with the non-participating Mediterranean States."

Jews are recognized in the Soviet Union as a national minority and Judaism is one of the recognized religions. There are clauses in the Final Act that ought to be conducive to better conditions for Soviet Jews to live as Jews in the USSR. And there is a section on "Travel for Personal and Professional Reasons" which, if fully and fairly implemented, should mean freedom for Soviet Jews to attend international Jewish conferences, at least those on religious subjects.

The Helsinki Declaration has been criticized for lacking legal force. But the fact that the Final Act is not legally binding does not make it valueless or unimportant. Political interest may be more powerful than moral, or even legal, force. The Final Act is an element in promoting detente, to which the Soviet Union attaches great value. The Soviet Union has, therefore, been very forthcoming with regard to the Act's juridical character. Party Secretary Brezhnev said in Helsinki that the Helsinki document must be "made a law of international life not to be breached by anyone." But he also added that "no one should try to dictate to other peoples...the manner in which they ought to manage their internal affairs," which reflects the consistent claim of the Communists that a State's practices in the domain of human rights are its domestic concern.

So far, the years since the Helsinki signature have brought little comfort to Soviet Jews, except for a slight reduction of the exit visa fee since January 1976. Those who wish to leave the USSR continue to suffer hardship and harassment. The Jewish "Prisoners of Conscience," whose only crime is their wish to join their families in Israel, have not been pardoned. Facilities for the exercise of Jewish religious life or culture have not been improved.

Note: Although the Soviet Union signed this declaration, they still deny the applicants who call upon the "Declaration of Human Rights" the free practice of their religion in the USSR. They also deny rights on emigration saying that it is an "internal affair." Furthermore, the Soviets have been violating the Helsinki Agreement's guarantee of freedom of contact by intercepting mail, especially the invitations sent to Soviet Jews from their relatives in Israel -- an indispensable document for requesting an exit visa.

*Taken from the information briefing pamphlet entitled *Jews in the Soviet Union,* published by the Israel Information Center.

NOTES

1. Keller, W., *Und Werden Zerstreut Unter Alle Voelker* (trans., And Will Be Dispersed Among All Nations). Germany: Knaur 1966, p. 488.
2. Schloss, R.W., *Lass Mein Volk Ziehen* (trans., *Let My People Go*). Munich, Germany: Olzog Verlag, 1971, p. 16.
3. Shifrin, A., *Das Verhoer* (trans., *The Interrogation*). Germany: Stephanus Verlag, 1977, p.148.
4. *Dokumente und Analyse* (trans., *Documents and Analyses*). Germany: March 1983, p.18.
5. *Ibid.*, p.122, p. 154.
6. Schloss, R.W., *op. cit.*, p.184.
7. *Aus Politik und Zeitgeschichte* (trans., *From Politics and History*). Germany: May 1982, p.40.
8. *Ibid.*, May 1982, p. 39.
9. *Allgemeine Juedische Wochenzeitung* (trans., *General Jewish Weekly*). Germany: March 4, 1983.
10. *Frankfurter Allgemeine Zeitung* (trans., *Frankfurt General News*). Germany: March 16, 1983.
11. *Braunschweiger Zeitung* (trans., *Braunschweig News*). Germany: November 12, 1982.
12. *Die Weltwoche* (trans., *The World Week*). Zurich, Switzerland: November 17, 1982.
13. Abosch, Heinz, *Antisemitismus in Russland* (trans., *Anti-Semitism in Russia*). Germany: Melzer Verlag, 1972, p. 54.
14. *Braunschweiger Zeitung* (trans. *Braunschweig News*). Germany: April 21, 1983.